THE
Rose
OF
Tralee

FIFTY YEARS A-BLOOMING

Right: Alice O'Sullivan, the first
Rose of Tralee, 1959 with
Aoife Kelly, Rose of Tralee 2008

DEDICATION:

To Mary Lu, Ken, Alwyn and Leah Merritt

ACKNOWLEDGEMENTS:

I would like to acknowledge the cooperation of *The Kerryman*, which kindly made all their photographs available for this book. Without the photographs taken over the years by staff photographer Kevin Coleman, the book would not have been possible. In that context I would like to thank the editor Declan Malone for making the pictures available and acknowledge the generosity of John Cleary in kindly agreeing to have his photographs included with *The Kerryman* pictures. Padraig Kennelly of *Kerry's Eye* and Tim Vaughan of the *Irish Examiner* also generously agreed to fill in some gaps, and Joe Hanley kindly made his pictures available. I would like to acknowledge Kerry County Librarian Tommy O'Connor and his staff, especially Olive Moriarty and Eddie Bailey, for their help. The selection of the photographs used in the book was entirely in the hands of Mary Webb, editor, and designer Emma Byrne of The O'Brien Press who did a magnificent job in preparing this book at extremely short notice. I would also like to thank Gay Byrne for introducing the book, and of course, my mother Margaret Dwyer, through whose contacts I enjoyed an inside view stretching through the five decades that the Rose of Tralee has bloomed.

TRD

Tralee, 2009.

Opposite right: Eleanor Carrick, Tralee Rose 1979,
who worked in the Festival Office for over twenty years

Cover back: The 2006 Roses. The winner, Kathryn Feeney from
Queensland is fourth from left.

THE

Rose
OF
Tralee

FIFTY YEARS A-BLOOMING

INTRODUCTION BY GAY BYRNE

T. RYLE DWYER

THE O'BRIEN PRESS
DUBLIN

Introduction

When I was first approached to host the Rose of Tralee competition in 1974, I must admit I had my doubts. A beauty pageant wasn't in my normal line of work, and I wasn't too sure what Kathleen Watkins would say about it!

The charm of the event was that the competitors could be anybody's daughter, sister, or niece. It was not a beauty competition, or a talent contest, but it did combine elements of each in what might be called a personality show. The winner was selected by the judges for possessing a mysterious quality typified by the line in the song —''twas not her beauty alone that won me'. The judges were looking for what the French would call that certain *je ne sais quoi*.

When the festival started in 1959 the jet age had not yet begun in terms of popular travel. People did not go to America for the weekend, as some tend to do now. Most emigrated to Britain, America, Australia, or New Zealand, but in a sense many never really left Ireland. They lived a sort of a half-life in as much as they were over there but part of them remained at home in Ireland. They mixed with Irish immigrants, socialised in Irish circles, and were members of Irish clubs. They had their daughters and sons learn Irish dancing and sing Irish songs.

They made a point of coming back to Ireland as regularly as possible to recharge their Irish batteries in a figurative sense. Then they went back and continued this half-life abroad.

They popularised Irish music, Irish dancing and the Irish pub abroad, to the extent that they were responsible for a renaissance of the music and dance of Ireland. It was in America that the Clancy Brothers and Tommy Makem first made their names, and they helped to popularise the folk music scene in Ireland. And it was a couple of Irish-Americans – Michael Flatley from Chicago and Jean Butler from New York – who did so much to popularise Irish dancing on the international stage as the original stars of Riverdance. They were a reminder not only that the Irish abroad but also their descendants are a national asset that should be treasured.

The Rose of Tralee is a celebration of young women born in Ireland and the foreign-born descendants of Irish people. In my twenty-five-year association with the festival, I found those young

Above: The Three Amigos. Van Morrison, Marty Whelan and Gay Byrne
Below: These will never fit!
Gay with Perth Rose, Michelle Dealtry
Across, from top: Gay shares a laugh with a 1978 Rose; Gay with Jessie Lyons, Kerry Rose 2003, and Grainne Casey, Manchester Rose 1986

ladies wonderful. They were full of personality and bounce, eager to display their singing, reciting, dancing – even coercing me into the act on a few memorable occasions! It was my job to help them to express their personalities.

As well as representing a good time – the hospitality, good comradeship, genuine fondness and so on – getting the show on the road in Tralee was also extremely hard work. Maura Connolly, my assistant on the 'Late Late Show', came down every year with me. What people didn't realise was that Maura and I sat in two rooms in the Brandon Hotel and she interviewed half of the girls while I interviewed the other half. There were often over thirty girls to be interviewed. That meant a tremendous amount of time and effort, making notes on each of the girls, doing our general research, advising them on what to say and do on stage, and all of that sort of thing.

The last year that I hosted the Rose of Tralee, it got a TV audience of 1.5 million – at twenty minutes past midnight on an August Tuesday! And that count was of home sets alone. We had no idea how many viewers we had in hotels, hospitals, pubs, clubs or elsewhere. Yet during the whole time I was involved as compere and judge, I cannot remember reading a good review of the programme in any Irish newspaper, with the sole exception of Eamon Dunphy in the *Sunday Independent*.

Looking back, what stood out most for me was the pride of the young women in their Irishness – whether they were from Cork or California. For some the Irish connection in their roots went way back to a dim and distant past of more than a century earlier. Their only tangible link might have been a faded photograph in the family album.

The Rose of Tralee affords an opportunity to celebrate and renew those links with Ireland. It was always wonderful to observe the parents in the audience, absolutely bursting with pride that their daughter should be representing their city, their state, or indeed their country.

The whole Festival was then, and continues to be, a joyous event that gives people from all over the world a chance to re-connect with their heritage. For me it was a highlight of the year and something I looked forward to enormously. I congratulate all of those who have nurtured it through the first fifty years, and wish it another fifty, and more.

Gay Byrne

A Rose is Crowned

The Dome is filled to overflowing – thousands of people who have sat through two nights of interviews, displays of talent, reminiscences about family histories. Sections of the audience are unashamedly partisan, rooting for the daughter, sister, granddaughter they have travelled many thousands of miles to support on her big night. Banners wave and the expectant hush is punctured by shouts of 'come on, California', 'up the Banner' or the like. Even the non-affiliated have by now chosen a favourite. The Roses gather on stage in a nervous group, some holding hands. This is, after all, known as the friendly competition, where girls have bonded over the past week, and will in some cases have made life-long friends. Then comes time for the announcement.

'The 2009 Rose of Tralee is ...' The television cameras capture incredulity on the face of the winner, a huge cheer from her family and friends, hugs of congratulation from her competitors. She walks forward and bends her head to receive the Philip Treacy-designed Newbridge Silver crown. Then the song begins. She already knows all the words but now they're being sung especially for her...

Across: Aoife Kelly, Rose of Tralee 2008, adjusts her crown
Above: Enthusiastic supporters carry the flag for their favourite
Below: Crowds enjoying the fun on the streets of Tralee

'The pale moon was rising above the green mountain
The sun was declining beneath the blue sea;
When I strayed with my love to the pure crystal fountain,
That stands in the beautiful Vale of Tralee.

She was lovely and fair as the rose of the summer,
Yet 'twas not her beauty alone that won me;
Oh no, 'twas the truth in her eyes ever dawning,
That made me love Mary the Rose of Tralee …

The cool shades of evening their mantle were spreading,
And Mary all smiling was listening to me;
The moon through the valley her pale rays were shedding,
When I won the heart of the Rose of Tralee.

In the far fields of India, 'mid war's dreadful thunders,
Her voice was a solace and comfort to me,
But the chill hand of death has now rent us asunder,
I'm lonely tonight for the Rose of Tralee
…'

Below: Roses gather at the Mulchinock home where Mary O'Connor, the inspiration for the song 'The Rose of Tralee' worked
Across: The pale moon rising over the bay, 1959

First Buds

The Rose of Tralee is now the highlight of a week-long international festival, bringing girls from the Irish Diaspora and their proud families back to the land from where their parents, grandparents, or great-grandparents emigrated so many years previously. But, back in 1958, when the idea was first conceived, few could have imagined that it would blossom into an event that attracts entrants from all over the world, with television viewing audiences in the millions.

In the 1950s Tralee had little industry and even that was in trouble. Whole families were uprooted and had to emigrate because of the lack of jobs. Something had to be done to attract tourists and boost the local economy.

In 1957 the Irish Racing Board decided to extend the town's annual two-day race meeting to three days and some local business people suggested holding a carnival at the same time. The centre of

Below: The races at Ballybeggan were an integral part of the Festival for many years

Top: Traditional dancers take part in the parade
Middle: Kathleen Sheehy, the Rose representing
Tralee in 1959
Bottom: Four of the original group of five who got
together in Harty's pub in 1958 and came up with
the idea for the Festival: Ned Nolan, Joe Grace,
Roger Harty, Florence O'Connor

Above: Beatrice Spring, Carnival Queen, 1957
Below: The 1939 pageant. Eithne O'Sullivan, seated centre, was selected Queen

attraction was the selection of a Carnival Queen. The concept was copied from a highly successful pageant held in 1939 when Eithne O'Sullivan of Valentia Island was selected queen. Beatrice Spring, a niece of the local Dáil Deputy Dan Spring, and first cousin of Dick Spring, future leader of the Labour Party, was the first new Carnival Queen.

One of the highlights of the second carnival in 1958 was a golf exhibition involving professionals Harry Bradshaw and Christy O'Connor. After the exhibition Bradshaw and O'Connor flew to Mexico City, where they won the prestigious Canada Cup, the World Golf Championship.

A group came together in Roger Harty's pub to talk about building on the success of the second carnival: Dan Nolan, publisher of *The Kerryman* newspaper, his half-brother, Ned, local butcher Florence O'Connor, along with Joe Grace, a solicitor and secretary of the local Race Company, and Roger Harty. They came up with the idea of developing on the Carnival Queen concept by exploiting the 19th century love song, 'The Rose of Tralee', which was written by a local merchant, William Pembroke Mulchinock. He had fallen in love with Mary O'Connor, a servant girl working for his family, who were bitterly opposed to the relationship. William was packed off to India in the Army to forget her, but he never did. When he returned, he learned that she had died, and he wrote the famous song.

Dan Nolan travelled to Boston in early October 1958 and received an enthusiastic response to the

Top: Roses make hay in 1962
Bottom: Maureen McCready, wife
of the noted rose grower who bred
a rose called Rose of Tralee and was
also a Rose selection judge for a
number of years

festival. Mike Reidy, a Kenmare expatriate, suggested the Festival of Kerry as an all-embracing title that would appeal to emigrants from throughout the county. Hence the Festival of Kerry was born. New York Mayor Robert Wagner told Dan Nolan that he would head a New York delegation to the festival.

Aer Lingus had inaugurated its transatlantic service to New York in April, so it was an ideal time to promote travel by attracting Irish emigrants home for a holiday. Ireland was also on the verge of a major change. Eamon de Valera stepped down from active politics following his election as President in June 1959. Seán Lemass replaced him as Taoiseach and set about invigorating the Irish economy with a major push towards industrialisation. The government began to recognise the importance of tourism, and the Festival of Kerry was designed to put Tralee on the tourist map.

From the outset the festival sought to capitalise on well-placed Kerry people in the civil service in Dublin, as well as Kerry emigrants who had been successful abroad. Many of those were eager to do something for their native county. The new festival provided an outlet for men like Brian K. Sheehy, a transport inspector in New York City; Billy Clifford in London, and John Byrne, who had recently been persuaded by Lemass to begin building in Dublin, after making his fortune in construction and dance halls in Britain.

The initial plan was for five young ladies to be selected as contestants, from New York, London, Birmingham, Dublin and

Above: Boston Rose, Alice O'Leary,
has her 'passport' stamped as she
enters the Kingdom of Kerry

Tralee. All had to be unmarried and have parents from the Tralee area. Dan Nolan went to the United States to line up people to handle the New York end of things.

The committee commissioned a 2.5ton emblem of a lighted red rose with green leaves, with the inscription, 'The Festival of Kerry' in white lights underneath. It cost over £200 out of the committee's £750 budget for the year. The sign was hung on the front of the Ashe Memorial Hall.

About 150 people travelled from New York for the Festival in the last week of August 1959. Mayor Wagner had to cancel because of the impending visit of the Soviet leader Nikita Khrushchev to New York. On arrival at Shannon airport, the first of the New York group was greeted by a convoy of some eighty cars from Tralee. The Mayor of Limerick, John Carew, TD, was there to welcome them, along with Michael Clancy, Chairman of Ennis Urban District Council. The visitors were treated to an Irish coffee reception and each was presented with an official-looking Kingdom of Kerry passport – supplied by Donal Browne, the State Solicitor! The mock passports were later stamped at the Feale Bridge by a uniformed customs officer as the cavalcade of cars entered Kerry.

When the cars reached Tralee, they were led through the streets by mounted horsemen, torchbearers, and four bands: St. Joseph's Boys Brass Band and Gill Brien's Band, along with the Laune Pipers Band, and the Millstreet Pipe Band. About 20,000 people lined the streets.

A second charter plane with some seventy-five people had to return to Gander in Newfoundland, Canada, due to engine trouble, and it did not arrive in Shannon until the following day. Many of these were coming especially for the unveiling of the new monument in Ballyseedy to commemorate the massacre of eight IRA volunteers killed during the civil war in March 1923.

While the festival committee had nothing to do with the Ballyseedy monument, the unveiling took place on the Sunday of the festival, and John Joe Sheehy, head of the monument organising committee, was also father of the young woman chosen to represent Tralee in the Rose contest. So the committee invited the overseas

Top: The original Rose emblem
Middle: Joe Grace, Secretary of Ballybegan, inspecting a jump
Bottom: The annual Rose photo taken at Shannon airport, 1983

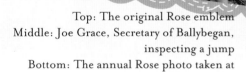

ROSES SHOW OFF THEIR TALENTS

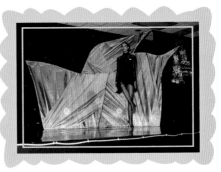

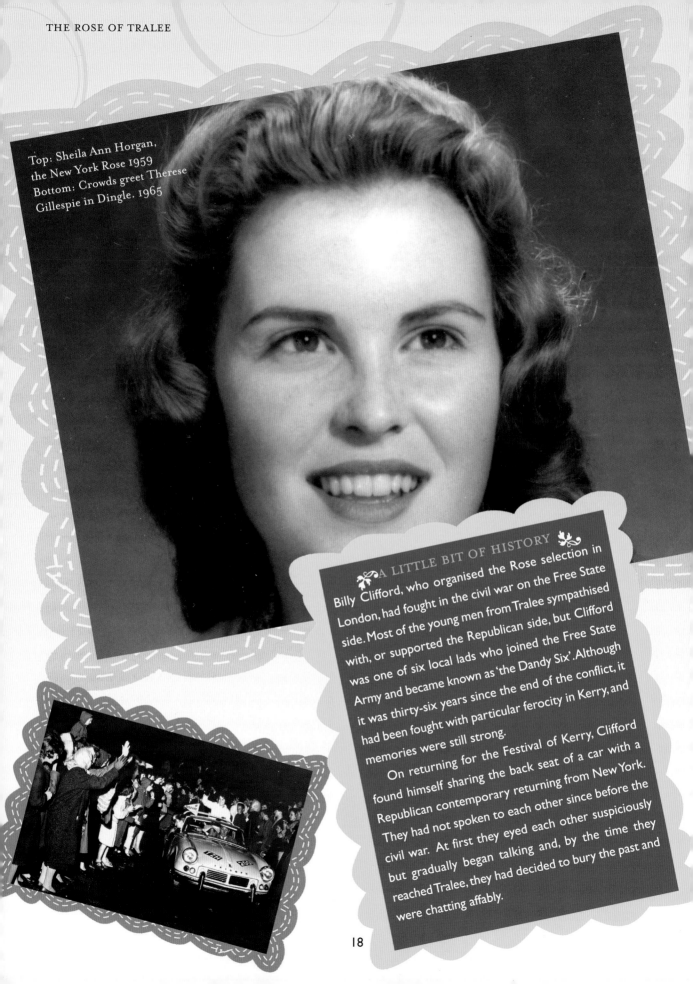

Top: Sheila Ann Horgan, the New York Rose 1959
Bottom: Crowds greet Therese Gillespie in Dingle. 1965

A LITTLE BIT OF HISTORY

Billy Clifford, who organised the Rose selection in London, had fought in the civil war on the Free State side. Most of the young men from Tralee sympathised with, or supported the Republican side, but Clifford was one of six local lads who joined the Free State Army and became known as 'the Dandy Six'. Although it was thirty-six years since the end of the conflict, it had been fought with particular ferocity in Kerry, and memories were still strong.

On returning for the Festival of Kerry, Clifford found himself sharing the back seat of a car with a Republican contemporary returning from New York. They had not spoken to each other since before the civil war. At first they eyed each other suspiciously but gradually began talking and, by the time they reached Tralee, they had decided to bury the past and were chatting affably.

Above: the five entrants for the 1959 competition. (from left) New York Rose Sheila Anne Horgan, London Rose Angela Flynn, Birmingham Rose Maura Browne, Kathleen Sheehy, the Tralee Rose and Alice O'Sullivan, the Dublin Rose

Below: Alice O'Sullivan, Rose of Tralee 1959

visitors to a banquet at St John's CYMS Hall. The Great Southern Hotel, Killarney, did the catering for some 300 people.

Tralee did not have the commercial infrastructure to cater for the influx of so many people. The town's small hotels had a total of 104 rooms and there were only 18 registered guest houses. The festival committee set up an accommodation bureau to enlist townspeople to take in paying guests for bed and breakfast. This was run from Caball's shop in Bridge Street, where beds were organised for some 1,500 visitors.

The selection of the first Rose of Tralee was made at a festival dance in the Ashe Memorial Hall. Sheila Anne Horgan was the New York Rose, Alice O'Sullivan the Dublin Rose, Maura Browne represented Birmingham, Angela Flynn was the London Rose, and Kathleen Sheehy represented Tralee. The latter three had been reared in Tralee, while the parents of the New York Rose came from Ballyroe. Kathleen Sheehy was a member of the famous footballing family. Her father, John Joe, had twice captained Kerry to All-Ireland glory, and her four brothers all played for Kerry. The five roses were interviewed by Kevin Hilton, a commercial traveller from Limerick who continued in that role for the next eight years. The judges were Michael Mulchinock, a great-grand-nephew of the man who wrote 'The Rose of Tralee'; Walter Smithwick, director of Smithwicks Brewery, Kilkenny; Frank Bandy of Rank Films of London; Terry O'Sullivan, a popular columnist with the *Evening Press*; and Lord Harrington, who was chosen because of his involvement in horse racing.

❦ THE FIRST ROSE ❦

Alice O'Sullivan was selected as the Rose of Tralee, 1959. The event was captured on closed circuit television and relayed to the other festival dance in the CYMS Hall. This was a novelty for the people of Tralee, as there was no TV reception in the area at that time. Through his contacts Dan Nolan had assembled a

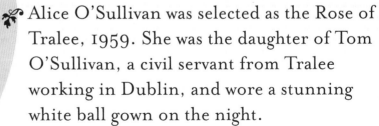

Alice O'Sullivan was selected as the Rose of Tralee, 1959. She was the daughter of Tom O'Sullivan, a civil servant from Tralee working in Dublin, and wore a stunning white ball gown on the night.

distinguished battery of the media in the Ashe Memorial Hall. They included camera crews from BBC, Twentieth-Century Fox, and International Newsfilms Ltd. 'The whole proceedings will be on television shortly,' Vincent Corcoran, the BBC cameraman told *The Kerryman*. 'In addition, sixteen copies of our film will be sent abroad. Over one hundred million TV viewers will see it abroad.'

Numerous competitions were arranged around the Festival. These included a Donkey Derby, a Tug-O-War competition, Tossing the Sheaf in the Town Park, a Terrier Derby in Rock Street, a bicycle race around the houses, swimming and kayak races in the canal. There was a handball competition in the Fitzgerald-Jones Alley. In addition, there was a children's race and a fancy dress parade for children. Of course, there were also three days of horse racing at Ballybeggan Park. The newly selected Rose of Tralee attended the final day's racing and presented prizes on behalf of the sponsors.

The great novelty item of that festival was a fireworks display. Almost fifty years later, when interviewed on the 'Tubridy Tonight' television programme, Alice O'Sullivan would remember the great crowd in Denny Street to witness the occasion and the 'terrific fireworks display'. People would have seen fireworks in movies, but most would never have seen a live display. There was also sheep dog demonstration in the Town Park by John Evans, who had brought over six dogs from Wales. Few of the sheep farmers in the hinterland had ever seen sheep dog trials. Some 80,000 people thronged into the town that night. This had an enormous impact on a town with a population of around 10,000.

At the race course the tote aggregate for the first day was up by over 66% and by 20% over the three days, so the Festival of Kerry had clearly been a success on many levels.

Above and below: Among the novelty events of the early festivals were the children's bicycle race and the donkey derby, both of which were hotly contested

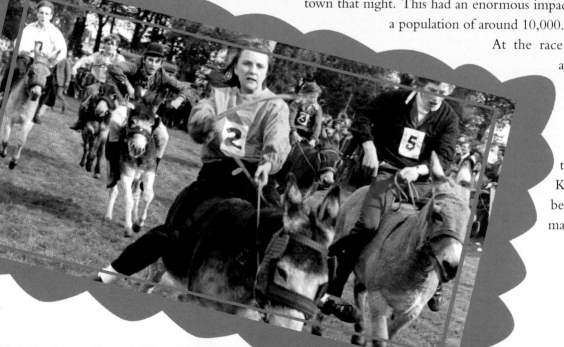

❦ THE SIXTIES ❦

Roger Harty went to New York in March 1960 to promote the second festival. Upon his return he was congratulated on his good work. 'I only done the best I could,' he replied modestly. Thereafter this became a kind of mantra within the festival committee.

In the second year the number of Roses was expanded to nine with the addition of representatives from Boston, Chicago, Leeds, as well as a Kerry Rose. Eligibility was extended to unmarried women with a parent from anywhere in Kerry, not just Tralee, and preliminary Rose dances were held throughout Kerry in the winter months, building up to a county final at which a young woman was chosen to represent the county. This enhanced the image of the festival as a countywide event.

The Rose of Tralee for 1960 was twenty-one-year-old Teresa Kenny.

🌿 The Rose of Tralee for 1960 was twenty-one-year-old Teresa Kenny.

The judges that year were Sean Keating of New York, Toddy O'Sullivan, the Managing Director of the Gresham Hotel, Dublin, Commander George Crosbie of the *Cork Examiner*, racehorse owner Rex Beaumont, and Walter Smithwick of the Kilkenny brewery.

A feature of the 1960 festival was the introduction of outdoor lighting. Purchased from Blackpool as surplus to their famous illuminations, they came in a variety of designs and colours, and, when erected along the fronts of business premises in the main street, they added greatly to the creation of a carnival atmosphere.

Events in 1960 included go-kart racing on a track that ran through the Town Park and onto the new road joining Denny Street and Princess Street. There was also a clay pigeon shoot and a drag hunt. In addition, the Kerry Fleadh Ceoil, a major Irish traditional music festival, with performances and competitions on fiddles, tin whistles, bodhráns and every other sort of instrument, as well as sean-nós singing and traditional Irish dancing, ran for three days during the festival.

Celebrations for the new Rose continued after the festival officially closed in Tralee on Thursday. Teresa Kenny visited Annascaul the following night for a dance, and went to her home town of Ballyheigue on Saturday night, where she

Above: Teresa Kenny, Rose of Tralee 1960
Below: All the entrants for the 1960 Rose selection. Teresa Kenny is second from left, standing

Top: As the festival grew in popularity, so did the crowds
Bottom: Roses pictured at Shannon airport in 1990

received a massive reception. The following week she was guest of honour at a dance in Ballybunion.

There were, however, some who had not been impressed by the festival's activities. Over the weekend, Dr Denis Moynihan, the Catholic Bishop of Kerry, publicly deplored the consumption of alcohol by young people on the streets of Tralee. 'I have been very sorry to hear,' Bishop Moynihan said, 'that during the recent festival in Tralee, quite a number of teenagers, boys and a few girls, were seen under the influence of drink on the streets of this town.'

At this time in Ireland, criticism from a member of the clergy, let alone a bishop, was taken very seriously indeed, as the influence of clerics on a population who were almost 100% practicing Roman Catholics was overwhelming. Even the highest politicians in the land would be considered very unwise to go against the clergy, unless, that is, they were unconcerned about retaining their seat in the next election. If the bishop publicly denounced the festival, it could kill it.

Indeed, the following year, publicans in Tralee had to go to the High Court to appeal for exemptions from the licensing laws for late night drinking during the festival. However, the issue revolved around the definition of a 'fair', and whether the festival could be considered a fair so that local pubs would be legally entitled to obtain exemptions. The bishop had nothing to do with this controversy, but his attitude would remain a matter for concern for some years.

During the winter months the festival committee again held heats in various dance halls throughout the county. A Kerry Rose was then selected from the winners in the various districts. It was a means of both publicising the festival and raising money, as the festival got a share of the dance takings.

Part of Aer Lingus's sponsorship involved all the Roses coming together at Shannon airport for a photo-call, so Roses from the US were met at the airport and then all the Roses together proceeded to Tralee in a cavalcade of some sixty cars. On the way, the cavalcade would stop at various towns to promote the festival.

Bertram Mills Circus, which claimed to be the largest circus in Europe, came to Tralee during the 1961 festival. It supplied animals and acts such as clowns, jugglers, and stilt walkers to

participate in a parade through the town each morning, along with the various bands. To have an elephant and a caged bear and tiger or lion parading through the town added great curiosity value to the proceedings. In the opening parade the elephant made a large 'deposit' at Moyderwell Cross, and those following had to tread carefully. Some wag suggested that this was the first roundabout in Tralee!

Novelty events that year included a demonstration by the Cytric Motor Cycling Team from London who gave an exhibition of tricks and grass track motor cycling skills in the Town Park. There was a gathering of Wren Boys – costumed men and boys who traditionally call to houses on St Stephen's Day, bringing the wren, originally a live bird, but more often nowadays a replica '– to give you a cheer, a Merry Christmas and a Happy New Year'. The National Pipe Band competition attracted bands from all over Ireland, as well as one from Birmingham.

Above and below: Elephants and kilted sword dancers added to the festivities

The ornate CIE State Carriage was a big draw. It was put on show at the railway station in Tralee for the week. Papal Legate Cardinal Agagianian was cited as its most famous passenger. He had travelled from Dublin to Cork in the carriage earlier in the year, and some apparently hoped that treating the carriage as a virtual relic might win favour with Bishop Moynihan and allow him to consider the festival in a more benign light!

It was a fun-packed week, with something for everyone: a variety concert on Denny Street, terrier racing, a dog show, the canal swim, sea angling in Tralee Bay, a children's tricycle race on Princess Street, children's roller skating races in Moyderwell and Denny Street, a barrel rolling contest in Railway Terrace, a 'Feathered Bird Show' at the CIE Hall in Staunton's Row and the all-Ireland junior football championship semi-final between Kerry and Louth played at the Austin Stack Park.

The Donkey Derby was a massive public attraction in the early years of the festival. Owners, jockeys and punters took the whole thing as seriously as the horse racing. There was, of course, the inevitable appearance of a 'five-legged donkey' - a donkey stallion who had been aroused by one of its female competitors. There would be enormous public amusement as the stallion tried to replace a competitor's jockey.

Five chartered flights came from the USA in 1961. The competition had now expanded to eleven Roses with the introduction of a Cork and a Limerick Rose. And indeed, it was one of these new entrants, Josie Ruane, from Cork, who stole the show and became the 1961 Rose of Tralee.

Josie Ruane, from Cork, who stole the show and became the 1961 Rose of Tralee.

✿ 1962 ✿

Fossett's Circus was set up in the Town Park in an open-air format in 1962. There was no charge for admission. Although they were particularly fortunate with the weather that year, the open-air format proved especially difficult for the tightrope walking and trapeze people because of the evening dew.

The various events around town were free, with the exception of the Rose selection dance at the Ashe Memorial Hall and the auxiliary dance at the CYMS Hall, once again linked to the selection by closed-circuit television. The price for entry was 7 shillings and 6 pence, equating to under 30 cents in current money.

The number of Roses in 1962 reached a perfect dozen, with the arrival of the San Francisco Rose. Elizabeth McCloy, whose grandparents were from Castleisland, flew to Ireland with the other three American Roses: Boston's Eta Slattery, Chicago's Kathleen Brosnan and New York's Myra Byrne.

THE ORIGINS OF THE FESTIVAL CLUB

A big hit at the first festival was a 'Winkle Party' which was held at the golf club, and featured shellfish. John Byrne, a native of Kilflynn, County Kerry who had become a successful builder abroad, had recently returned to Ireland with plans to build O'Connell Bridge House in Dublin. He was honoured by being invested as the 'Grand Winkler', with a chain of office made of seashells.

In 1960 the Winkle Party became a victim of the previous year's success. A horde of gatecrashers descended on the clubhouse at Mounthawk. When they could not get in the doors, they climbed through windows, including the kitchen window in the steward's residence. In 1961 a Festival Club was created as a replacement for the Winkle Party. Barney O'Connor, a former publican and a member of the festival committee, organised a bar in the Forester's Hall in Staughton's Row. Various drink companies were approached for product and they supplied cases of liquor and barrels of stout and beer. A certain amount of drink was allotted to each night to ensure that it would last for the entire festival. All drink was free in the Festival Club. The brandy would run out first, then the spirits, and finally the beer and stout. People's choice of free drink seemed to be determined largely by how much it would have cost them normally. Needless to say, the Festival Club, which did not open until 1 am when the local bars were officially shut, proved hugely popular.

Across: Josie Ruane, Rose of Tralee
1961, with Joe Lynch
This page, top: A surprised Ciara
O'Sullivan, Rose of Tralee 1962
Middle: Ted Keane,
Gerry O'Leary,
Michael McNamara
and Emmett Kennelly
count the takings
Bottom:
The 1961 Roses
at Shannon
airport

However, Shannon airport was fog-bound, so the plane had to land in Dublin and the Roses then had to travel to Limerick by train in order to take part in the obligatory Shannon photo-shoot.

The winner was seventeen-year-old Ciara O'Sullivan of Dublin.

The winner was seventeen-year-old Ciara O'Sullivan of Dublin. A member of the National Ballet, she was a particularly popular choice. Her parents were born in Listowel. Ciara later married John Byrne, the builder and property developer. Shortly afterwards he was instrumental in building the Mount Brandon Hotel, which greatly facilitated putting Tralee on the tourist map and would play host to the Rose Ball in later years.

One of those who visited the festival from New York that year was Mike McGlynn, an old Republican who had fought in the War of Independence and ensuing Civil War. He asked if some of the Festival Committee would join him for dinner at Áras an Uachtaráin with his old friend, President Eamon de Valera. Florence O'Connor, Ned Nolan and Arthur J. O'Leary were duly invited. The local Fianna Fáil deputy, Tom McEllistrim, Snr., had never been to the Áras, so he was also invited.

'I suppose they are all ours,' de Valera said to McEllistrim.

'Yes, Chief,' McEllistrim replied, looking somewhat askance at O'Leary, who was chairman of the local Fine Gael party! Afterwards, de Valera had them shown around the Áras. As they were leaving, he asked if they had seen the guest room.

'You know,' he said, 'Princess Grace and five cardinals slept there.'

'Oh my God,' Arthur O'Leary quipped, 'not at the same time, I hope.'

It is not recorded whether this raised a laugh from the rather strait-laced First Citizen!

❧ 1963 ❧

The fame of the Rose of Tralee was reaching ever more far-flung fields and 1963 saw the arrival of a Rose from Sydney, Australia. Along with a new Rose from Coventry, this brought the number of entrants to fourteen.

That year the festival included a veteran car rally, and the vehicles were used to carry the Roses in some style in the opening parade. More than thirty cars were involved. They included a 1901 De Dion, a 1914 Rolls Royce, a 1914 Ford Model T, a 1923 Chevrolet and a 1929 Studebaker.

Geraldine Fitzgerald of Boston was chosen as the Rose of Tralee. Joe Landers, the festival organiser in Boston, later admitted that her selection as the Boston Rose had caused him considerable embarrassment because she was his wife's niece. He was, therefore, particularly relieved when she won in Tralee, as this vindicated her selection in Boston and removed any hint of a 'fix' on his part.

Geraldine Fitzgerald of Boston was chosen as the Rose of Tralee.

Nightly dances at the Ashe Memorial Hall and the CYMS were money spinners for the festival committee until 1963, when the CYMS ran its own festival dances. That year the popular Festival Club moved to the much more spacious Theatre Royal. The overall cost of the Festival Club, comprising the wages of three barmen, a steward, caretaker, rent of the hall and chairs, along with the decorating of the hall and all the drink, which was still given out free, came to less than £200!

Fossett's Circus had been free from the beginning, but then it was discovered that some canny kids were staying right through from the afternoon opening until the circus closed at night, meaning that other children couldn't get in. It was then decided to charge a one shilling entrance fee, with the money being donated to the local St Vincent de Paul society for charitable purposes.

You could argue that the still popular ballad group, the Wolfe Tones, got their 'start' at the 1963 festival, when their performance in The Tavern, owned by Derry O'Rourke, was broadcast on RTÉ radio, the first time they were played on air. Donnacha Ó Dulaing, who continues to have a loyal radio following at home and abroad for his weekly programme 'Fáilte Isteach' devoted one of his Munster Journal programmes to the festival. Much of the programme was taped in Tralee, where he recorded the Wolfe Tones. Ironically, they were singing 'The Sash', the unofficial anthem of Northern Unionists, which celebrates King Billy's victory at the Boyne and the sash worn by Orangemen during the annual Twelfth of July march. A radio

Across, top: Geraldine Fitzgerald, Rose of Tralee 1963
Middle and Bottom: Vintage cars were used to carry Roses in the 1963 parade
Above: The Wolfe Tones first performed at the festival in 1963. Their 1984 open-air concert drew this massive crowd, estimated at 30,000 people

critic in one of the national newspapers commented that he 'found it extraordinary to hear a group of young men with rather pronounced Dublin accents singing "The Sash" in the Deep South!'

Many people used to come down from Belfast for the festival, and they were stunned to find that 'The Sash', was particularly popular in the south. At the nightly singsongs in the pubs and hotels someone would inevitably launch into the song and most of the crowd would join in enthusiastically. Initially horrified, the Northern visitors would eventually sing along too, remarking that nobody was going to believe their story when they got home. Of course, this was before the Troubles erupted in Northern Ireland, and there was little understanding in Kerry of the sectarian problems north of the border.

The Wolfe Tones were such a success in 1963 that the festival committee decided to introduce three other musical competitions the following year. There were prizes for the best cabaret act, the best street entertainment (essentially a busking competition), and the Guinness International Folk Award for best folk group. The folk competition was held in public and was won by Teddy Furey and his three sons, with Finbar giving a virtuoso performance on the uileann pipes. The sons later became internationally famous as The Furey Brothers.

After the festival ended in Tralee, the Roses were guests at a dance in Listowel on Friday, Kilgarvan on Sunday, and the winning Rose was guest of honour at a dance in Brosna the following Wednesday.

❦ 1964 ❦

A press conference was held in July to publicise the 1964 festival. Florence O'Connor paid glowing tributes to both Bord Fáilte [the Irish tourist Board] and Guinness for their assistance, and Guinness came on board as a major sponsor, a situation that continued for three decades, until 2000.

However, costs were increasing all the time, and in 1964 the organising committee threatened to call off the festival if the traders of Tralee did not increase their contribution and provide around £2,000 of the £10,000 that was needed to run the Festival of Kerry, which was now billing itself modestly as 'The Greatest Free Show on Earth'.

The festival was lucky to have the participation and understanding of Michael Greeley, manager of the National Bank, which was later absorbed by the Bank of Ireland. He had been transferred to Tralee shortly before the second festival and became actively involved.

'The Greatest Free Show on Earth' was a worry to him as the committee had very little income other than from dances and small sponsorship. 'The four banks between them, after pressure, donated 2 guineas (almost €1.69) each,' he explained. Even then, that was a derisory sum for a bank. But he himself was hugely supportive when it came to loans and overdrafts. There was no formal arrangement for a fixed overdraft, but 'during the first few years I arranged sums between £500 and £2,000. I never asked for any security and nobody was ever anxious to sign a guarantee. I relied completely on the integrity of the members who came to visit me from year to year.' It was a relationship that worked very well.

Michael Greeley was a good judge of character. He funded a number of very successful businesses in Tralee by trusting their proprietors with loans at a time when the banks seemed prepared to loan money only to people who did not need it. He was also a man who knew how to enjoy himself. On one memorable occasion he attended a law society dinner at Benner's Hotel – an all-male affair on a Saturday that inevitably went on until the early hours of the following day. Some of the revellers, Michael among them, poured from the hotel into the parish church next door for 7 o'clock mass on the Sunday morning. Michael was at the back of the church with his arm draped around one of the angels that held up the holy water font. When Monsignor D.A. Reidy finished his sermon, Michael, perhaps thinking

Above and Below: Novelty events continued to attract the crowds
Across, top: Margaret O'Keeffe, Rose of Tralee 1964
Bottom: Horse-draw caravans were hired for the folk groups

he was still listening to one of the worthies from the law society, clapped enthusiastically and shouted for more. It was probably the best response the surprised Monsignor ever had to one of his homilies, and the incident was the talk of the town for some days.

The town collection in 1964 came to £1,600, which was up 60% on the previous year.

For the first time, a one-hour special television programme on the arrival of the Roses in Tralee was filmed. It got mixed reviews. 'The fourteen potential Roses of Tralee arriving in camera range, one by one, in closed cars, was a tedious and monotonous performance, said Ken Gray in *The Irish Times*. 'One pitied Larry Gogan who had to try to make it sound interesting and exciting.'

The winner that year was the Tralee Rose, Margaret O'Keeffe, the only time in the first fifty contests that the local entrant won. She used the victory as a springboard to become an airline stewardess with Aer Lingus.

The winner that year was the Tralee Rose, Margaret O'Keeffe

Adding to its list of titles, the festival now also billed itself as 'The Folk Festival of Ireland'. A folk village was formed in the town park for musicians who wished to take part in various music contests and they were given the use of horse-drawn tourist caravans that had been hired for the week. The village was the suggestion of Dermot Kenny, one of the festival committee, who got the idea from a visit to the World Fair in New York the previous October.

✾ 1965 ✾

It was generally agreed that the 1965 Festival was the most successful yet, even though it was held during a national newspaper strike, so there was only local press coverage, but the selection of the Rose of Tralee was actually televised live for the first time that year. It was held in the open air on a stage constructed on the front steps of the Ashe Memorial Hall.

By now the number of Roses had swollen to fifteen, as Canada was added to the growing list of countries who participated. Toronto Rose, Eileen Kearney, was their representative.

Therese Gillespie of Belfast was chosen as the Rose of Tralee. She later married Tim Collins, a local hotel owner, and settled in

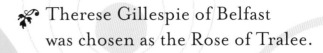

**Therese Gillespie of Belfast
was chosen as the Rose of Tralee.**

Tralee. Part of her prize was a three-week coast-to-coast tour of the United States during which she promoted the Festival of Kerry.

1966

From the beginning, the festival and the Ballybeggan races had run concurrently, the afternoon races being a big attraction for many during that week. In 1966, however, the race committee fixed their events for a week later than usual, and the festival committee had already set its dates by the time it found out.

In order the fill the void, the festival committee arranged for Fossett's Circus to put on a matinee each afternoon. A two-day horse trotting meeting was held in the Town Park and the sixteen Roses were collected from the Grand Hotel and ferried individually down to the park on a sulky. Some of the country's top horses competed in a gymkhana, with Tommy Wade, a distinguished international rider, winning the main event.

For the first time, there was an air display, featuring planes, gliders, helicopters and parachute jumping. The whole thing got a massive injection of publicity on the Sunday when John Byrne, who was due to be a judge at the Rose selection, crashed and wrecked his four-seater plane at the new grasslanding strip on Ballybeggan race course. The plane ended up ploughing through a ten-foot high wall, but John suffered only a broken arm. Suitably plastered, he proceeded to take his place among the judges.

There was no Australian Rose this year, but New Zealand was represented for the first time, by Loraine Stollery, who went on to be selected as Rose of Tralee.

The folk music theme continued, with special guests Heimatzunft Huffingen, a German folk group in traditional costume from the Black Forest. The group consisted of dancers, singers and a brass band. Their attendance was arranged by Gunther Beckers, the

**Loraine Stollery, who went on to be
selected as Rose of Tralee**

German Cultural Attache. German Ambassador, Dr. Heinz von Truetzchler, attended the festival.

Guinness donated £560 in prize money for the folk events, which were divided into four sections, the highlight being the 'Come All Ye' competition, which involved fourteen ballad groups from all over Ireland and one from the Channel Islands. The prize included a recording contract, a TV test, and an engagement in a London ballroom, plus £100. Between 4,000 and 5,000 people gathered to witness the final on the platform on the steps of the Ashe Memorial Hall.

The International Folk Award Contest proved a triumph for veteran folk musician Teddy Furey, who saw his three sons carry off the premier honours.

❦ 1967 ❦

Eligibility for the contest was extended in 1967 to young women of any Irish ancestry, rather than restricted to Kerry origins.

There was a feeling that the festival itself was beginning to grow stale. Florence O'Connor summed it up well: 'The organisation was founded to put life into Tralee during the week of Tralee Races … Our objective was simply defined and created no great problems. We discovered that dedication and hard work could make what seemed to be impossible reasonable and within our power. The first festivals were fired by the enthusiasm of a committee determined to prove that it could create a super festival. Having more or less achieved this purpose … the old crusading spirit seemed to tire and the momentum of the Festival slackened.'

A new lease of life was injected into the festival committee with the decision to introduce floral floats. These proved expensive to make because they were decorated with real flowers. But, because there was no precedent for these floats in Ireland, it was exactly the challenge that appealed to the Festival of Kerry committee, proving, as O'Connor commented, 'There was life in the old dog yet.'

The floats were made by festival members and the staff of two local factories – Traly Footwear and Kerry Precision Ball. They were a big success and lent extra colour and excitement to the Rose parade.

One of the features at the festival dances in 1967 was the appearance of the singing priest, Fr. Michael Cleary. He was particularly welcome as there had been a controversy over a scheduled appearance of the busty starlet Jayne Mansfield at Mount Brandon Ballroom back in April.

ROSES THROUGH THE YEARS

33

Bishop Moynihan and Monsignor John Lane, the Dean of Kerry, both denounced her appearance. In Killarney the following message was read out at all masses: 'Our attention has been drawn to an entertainment at Tralee tonight. The bishop requests you not to attend.'

'A woman is brought here to give a show for which she is being paid £1,000,' Dean Lane announced in Tralee. 'This woman boasts that her New York critics said of her, "she sold sex better than any performer in the world". I appeal to the men and women, to the boys and girls of Tralee, to dissociate themselves from this attempt to besmirch the name of our town for the sake of filthy gain. I ask all our people to ignore the presence of this woman and her associates. They are attempting something that is contrary to the moral teaching of our faith, that is against our traditions and against the ordinary decencies of life, something that is against everything we hold dear.' He went so far as to say that the entrance of this woman to the town was a slur on the annual Festival of Kerry when, for a few days, they selected someone whom they considered expressed the ideal womanhood, and called 'Rose of Tralee'.

The management of the Mount Brandon Hotel duly cancelled Mansfield's appearance, but the episode made international news, and it continued to stir controversy in Ireland during the following weeks. The Tralee Vocational Education Committee formally protested over a skit about the affair on Gay Byrne's 'Late Late Show', and the issue was still provoking letters to the national newspapers when Mansfield was tragically killed in a car accident in the United States on 29 July 1967.

There was a record eighteen Roses in 1967, with new Roses from Liverpool and Galway. Limerick Rose Geraldine Healy was a daughter of Eithne O'Sullivan Healy, the first Carnival Queen back in 1939. Ann Foley of Birmingham was chosen as Rose of Tralee. Part of her prize included an invitation to the Rose Festival in Tyler, Texas. On the way she stopped off in Washington to visit the White

THE ORDER OF THE GOLDEN ROSE

In order to boost the morale of those in its world-wide network, the Festival of Kerry introduced the Order of the Golden Rose to give special recognition to those who had proved helpful to the festival over the years. Men were presented with gold cufflinks and women with a gold pin, both with the rose motif. These were treasured and the recipients would usually wear them during formal occasions in Tralee. Among the first to receive the Golden Rose was Dan Nolan, the first President of the Festival. Other recipients came from Denmark, New Zealand and the United States.

🌹 Ann Foley of Birmingham was chosen as Rose of Tralee.

House and presented a Waterford Crystal bowl to Lady Bird Johnson, wife of President Lyndon B. Johnson.

🌿 1968 🌿

Terry Wogan replaced Kevin Hilton as compere of the Rose Selection in 1968. Born in Limerick, he had joined RTÉ in the early 1960s and began broadcasting on BBC in 1967. He hosted the Rose Selection in 1968, '69 and 1970.

The other big news in 1968 was the addition of six new Roses: French Rose Georgina Girassi, 19, a university student from Paris, Deirdre O'Reilly from Los Angeles, Philadelphia Rose Ann O'Reilly, Nottingham Rose Moira O'Connell, and two new Irish Roses – Eileen Slattery from Clare and Marion Nagle from Waterford. Of these, the Rose who travelled the shortest distance emerged the winner: Clare Rose Eileen Slattery, who was a singer in Bunratty Castle.

🌹 Clare Rose Eileen Slattery, was a singer in Bunratty Castle.

Terry Wogan's wife, Helen, accompanied him to the Rose Selection in 1968. He wrote about it in his autobiography, *Is it Me?*: 'The local committee saw to our every need, and took us to the festival club, where the elite would converse like decent people over a pint of stout.' There was some music there and this 'led to the odd song and some spirited dancing'.

'Would you care to dance?' a young lad asked Helen.

'No thank you,' she replied. 'I am talking with my friends.'

'Ah, well,' the young lad replied, much to Terry's amusement, 'you're too old for me anyway.'

🌿 1969 🌿

One of the judges in 1969 was Countess Lily McCormack, widow of tenor John McCormack, whose beautiful rendition of the song helped to make 'The Rose of Tralee' so famous. There were twenty-three Roses this year, with new entrants from Argentina,

Across, top: The Waterford Glass Rose trophy
Bottom: Recipients of the Golden Rose in 1972: Batt McCarthy, Murt O'Shea, Mary Rose Teahan, Dan Nolan, Billy Clifford, John Daniels and Harry Milner
Above, from top: Ann Foley, Rose of Tralee 1967; Eileen Slattery, Rose of Tralee 1968 with compere Terry Wogan and Festival President Michael Maye

Melbourne and Holyoke, Massachusetts. Marta Elena McLoughlin from Argentina, the first Latin American Rose, was the big public curiosity.

The twenty-three Roses were flown from Shannon to Farrenfore airport in an airplane piloted by Aidan Lawford, manager of Shannon Flying Services. The flight was timed to coincide with the official opening of the new airport by the Minister for Transport and Power, Brian Lenihan on August 30, 1969. He performed the ceremonial opening by cutting the tape to release the windsock.

Members of the cast of the movie 'Ryan's Daughter', which was being filmed on location in Kerry, were conspicuous at the festival that year. The Roses were invited on to the set to meet with stars Robert Mitchum, Trevor Howard and John Mills.

Another visitor to the festival that year was Maeve Binchy, then an *Irish Times* columnist, but later to become a worldwide bestselling novelist. She obviously enjoyed her Kerry experience.

'I think it would be hard not to enjoy Tralee,' she wrote on the front page of *The Irish Times*. 'It is full of incident and surprise. The very first morning a brass band plays music under your window, at such a pitch that you have to sit up in bed and wonder are you dead and in hell. If you go out quietly to buy a packet of cigarettes the shop could be full of mummers or biddy boys, with masks and great lumps of straw sticking out of them.'

'Literally everyone who came here is having a good time, and if that sort of thing doesn't bring people to Ireland in these difficult days, it is quite impossible to know what will,' Binchy remarked. Such reporting was a far cry from the early days of the festival when any reports were short, and buried in one of the inside pages.

'The Rose is chosen as much on her personality as seen over three days as on physical appearance on stage,' Maeve continued. 'There were 1,000 prized places in the hall, but over 100,000 waited on Denny Street and in the Square for the result.'

The result in 1969 was that Dublin Rose Cathy Quinn became the Rose of Tralee.

The result in 1969 was that Dublin Rose Cathy Quinn became the Rose of Tralee

❦ THE SEVENTIES ❦

In the midst of the growing troubles in Northern Ireland, the Festival of Kerry was taking on national significance in helping to promote tourism.

'Tralee offers more entertainment for its size than any other place in Ireland,' Eamonn Ceannt, the Director General of Bord Fáilte, told the Guinness press conference to publicise the 1970 festival. Cathy Quinn, the 1969 Rose, had visited Miami, Spain and Cyprus during preceding months.

'There was even a suggestion yesterday that the Rose of Tralee might become a full-time job as Ireland's ambassadress to the world,' according to the writer of the Irishman's Diary in *The Irish Times*. 'You must admit that in these improbable times stranger things have happened.'

Two new American centres participated in the 1970 festival – Miami and Michigan, and the eventual winner also came from the US. She was Kathleen Welsh from Holyoke, Massachusetts, whose great grandmother was a Moriarty from Tralee. It was a surprise for Kathleen who said she thought her room-mate in the Mount Brandon Hotel, Evelyn Barden (Dublin) would win. Minister Brian Lenihan introduced the new Rose of Tralee to the crowds outside the Ashe Memorial Hall, following a fanfare of trumpets from the Army Band of the Southern Command.

❧ Kathleen Welsh from Holyoke, Massachusetts was the winner

That year the festival hired its first full-time secretary, Jim Casey. In the midst of the personnel changeover a comparatively large debt was incurred and it was necessary to cut back on some of the events, such as the float parade.

Florence O'Connor had effectively been the driving inspiration of the festival since 1960 when he took over as chairman. Dan Nolan remained as President through 1963, when O'Connor officially became President. Ted Keane, Snr., succeeded him in 1967 and Michael Maye in 1968, but people still looked to O'Connor for guidance, and he became President again in 1969 and 1970. After the 1970 Festival he decided to step back completely and in October

Across from top: Countess McCormack with Tralee Rose Ann O'Mahony and French Rose Martine Brohan; Maeve Binchy (centre) with Trevor Howard and Cathy Quinn; Rose of Tralee 1969, Cathy Quinn waves to the audience
This page: Brian Lenihan with Kathleen Welsh, Rose of Tralee 1970

A LITTLE BIT OF HISTORY

Brian Lenihan, the Fianna Fáil Minister, opened the festivities that year in the midst of a good deal of political intrigue.

Finance Minister Charles Haughey had been arrested on charges of attempted gunrunning and was still awaiting trial during the festival, but he came down to the race meeting along with his father-in-law, former Taoiseach Seán Lemass. Justice Minister Des O'Malley was also present, though he managed to avoid the photographers. Lenihan and O'Malley had secret meetings with Haughey in Tralee, much to the chagrin of the Secretary of the Department of Justice, who had Haughey under surveillance. These events were to have repercussions in official circles for many years.

1970 New York-born Margaret Dwyer was elected the first woman President of the Festival of Kerry.

Dwyer's mother was from Tralee, and her father was a New Yorker. She had visited Tralee after graduating from high school, and then again in 1948 with her two young children. Her husband had been killed fighting in Germany during World War II, and she decided that Tralee was the place to set up home for her family.

'It's a big challenge for anyone and a bigger challenge for me because I am a woman,' she told *The Kerryman*.

One of the first things to be tackled was the poor financial situation. 'I'm determined to find plenty of sponsors so that there is enough money to do what we want for the next festival,' Margaret announced.

As a New Yorker promoting an Irish festival, Margaret Dwyer got ready access to the media in Canada and the United States. She also had discussions with American travel agents about the possibility of setting up Rose committees in Missouri, and Spokane, Washington.

This enhanced the festival's influence within Bord Fáilte and Aer Lingus, who were keen to support any initiative that would help reduce the damage done by the Northern troubles to tourism in the rest of the country. Because Ireland was so small, people abroad assumed that the violence was countrywide and it became very important to reassure them that the Republic was largely free of the Northern troubles. This is where Roses from various centres abroad played a kind of ambassadorial role.

Below: The Roses and Festival President Margaret Dwyer (in white trench coat) in front of the 'Rose of Tralee' Cessna
Across, from top: Linda McCravy, Rose of Tralee 1971 with compere Brendan O'Reilly and Margaret Dwyer; Linda on stage following her selection; Bishop Eamonn Casey, Linda and Margaret Dwyer

🌿 1971 🌿

For the first time ever the overseas Roses would fly into Dublin, instead of Shannon, in an attempt to exploit coverage in the national media. As a further promotional gimmick it was decided that Margaret Dwyer should fly to Dublin from Farrenfore in a small Cessna plane owned by Kerry Airways and renamed The Rose of Tralee for the occasion. The tactic worked, and the arrival of the Roses in Dublin was covered by all the national daily newspapers, as well as the two Dublin evening papers.

Accommodation in Dublin was provided courtesy of the Gresham Hotel, and the Roses traveled to Tralee by special bus, with planned stops at Portlaoise, Nenagh, and Limerick. There was one unplanned stop just outside Dublin, where the Garda Síochána flagged down the bus. Everyone was asked to get out for a photograph, but the real reason was so that the police could search the bus, as a bomb warning had been received. This turned out to be a hoax. At Patrickswell the more traditional motorcade was initiated, with scheduled stops in Abbeyfeale and Castleisland.

Margaret Dwyer was supposed to fly back to Farrenfore on the small plane, but Kerry airport was fogbound and they had to land at Shannon. It was a hair-raising experience – a transatlantic plane had to be diverted as the air traffic controller announced that he lost the small plane on radar.

The mantle of compere passed from Terry Wogan to Brendan O'Reilly of RTÉ in 1971, and the number of Roses reached a record twenty-six. In addition to Calgary and Lawrence from North America, there were also two new British centres: Newcastle and Thames Valley. A Bristol Rose had also been chosen during an Irish Week run by the Four Provinces Club, but she changed jobs shortly after and there was difficulty in contacting her about travel arrangements. She did eventually make it to Tralee, but the festival had already begun, so judges decided not to consider her, which sparked a brief controversy in the media. Linda McCravy from Miami was selected as the 1971 Rose of Tralee.

The entertainment for the festival included variety shows headed by Jack Cruise and Jack O'Connor, appearing each night on one of the two stages on the streets. There were the usual daily parades, bands, folk groups and dance troupes. Crowds of up to 100,000 thronged the town each night.

❧ Linda McCravy from Miami was selected as the 1971 Rose of Tralee.

Seamus Kelly of Quidnunc fame in *The Irish Times* described it thus:

'… a bewildering experience, requiring the constitution of an ox. All over Tralee there are temporary street theatres where the people can come and look at German folk dancers, Hession Troupe from Galway, or the Killingsworth Sword Dancers, or the Newcastle Kingsmen, or Punch and Judy shows, or ventriloquists, or any of the umpteen variety shows, all free. If that palls, there is the City of London Girl Pipers, the New York Police Department Pipe Band, Fossett's Famous Circus, and a Fun Fair featuring a Big Dipper called,

grandly, La Souris.'

Going into pubs in Tralee was 'like trying shoulder one's way out through a crowd after a Croke Park final,' wrote Terry O'Sullivan in the *Evening Press*. 'Every pub was a club, every place was full, full of the sound of Kerry talk, full of the smell of fried onions and hot fat from the mobile canteen that drifted in so smugly under the street lights.'

As a visitor to the festival for the first time, Gus Smith of the *Sunday Independent* was 'deeply impressed by the "free show" aspect of it. Well organised and enjoyable variety and theatre shows were presented on improvised stages in the streets and the shows were immensely enjoyed by thousands.'

The festival came to a rather premature end when the forty-five minute fireworks closing display had to be called off due to heavy rain. As a neighbourly gesture, the festival committee gave the £4,000 worth of fireworks to Listowel for their Harvest Festival later that month. However, when some children were injured by a firework at the Listowel event, the Festival of Kerry was successfully sued, adding to the company's growing insurance costs. As a result, the festival tended to focus more firmly on Tralee, to the exclusion of the rest of the county. Gradually it developed more as the Rose of Tralee Festival than the Festival of Kerry.

Financially, the 1971 festival was a particular success. Having cleared its back debts, it ended up overdrawn by just £52, but with £132 owed to the committee, according to treasurer Tom Hennebery. The total spend was £17,616, but, if one includes the sponsorship of various events, the total cost was around £45,000. A far cry from the £750 budget of the first festival committee in 1959! The banks in Tralee estimated the festival brought around £400,000 into the town that year.

This page: Young and old enjoyed the fireworks and street entertainment
Across from top: Taoiseach Jack Lynch meets with the 1972 Roses; A floral shoe float takes centre of attention; Roses at the crossroads have their Kerry passports checked

❦ 1972 ❦

The killing of fourteen civilians in Derry on Bloody Sunday, 30 January 1972, and the subsequent burning of the British Embassy in Dublin made world headlines. In terms of Irish tourism, it seemed likely that the 1972 season would be particularly bleak. Eamonn Ceannt, Director General of Bord Fáilte, arranged with Margaret Dwyer to have the 1971 Rose, Linda McCravy, do some promotional work on behalf of Bord Fáilte. Linda returned to Ireland in May

1972 for a two-week tour of the country and a visit to Britain with Margaret Dwyer. They attended the Rose selection dances in Dublin and Waterford, as well as functions in Birmingham and London.

Brendan O'Reilly was to host the Rose of Tralee again in 1972 but he had to withdraw in order to cover the Olympic Games in Munich. He was replaced by another television personality, Michael Twomey, a Cork comedian who had achieved countrywide fame as part of the Cha and Miah double act on the hugely popular 'Hall's Pictorial Weekly' TV show.

In order to boost the publicity surrounding the arrival of the Roses in Dublin, it was decided to try to arrange an audience for them with President Eamon de Valera, but this request was rejected on the grounds that such a meeting would be inappropriate – a strange response from a man whose stated vision of Ireland included 'comely maidens dancing at the crossroads'! However, Taoiseach Jack Lynch readily agreed. A photo opportunity was arranged with the Roses in the Taoiseach's office, and thereafter meeting the Taoiseach of the day became a regular feature.

Having successfully exploited the popularity of the folk music boom, the festival expanded its efforts to appeal to the broader Irish Diaspora. A federation of Kerryman's Associations was set up at the Earl of Desmond Hotel on the opening night of the Festival. Its patrons were Eamonn Casey, then Catholic Bishop of Kerry, and Charles Gray-Stack, the Protestant Dean of Ardfert, two very community-minded clerics. Some 200 people representing different centres came for the formation of the new federation. They included a group of seventy from London. Bishop Casey, who had spent much of his ministry working among Irish emigrants in Britain, praised the festival for drawing people together and creating bonds with emigrants.

Notwithstanding the almost total destruction of the tourist season around the country, a great crowd turned up in Tralee for the festival. Speaking to Tom Hennigan of the *Evening Herald*, Margaret Dwyer reported that 'There hasn't been a bed available for festival week for the past three weeks.' The festival had already arranged bookings for some

700 visitors from the United States. This included the 128 boys and girls of the South Hedley Tiger Marching Hundred, a high school band from Massachusetts. They had raised the money to pay their own fares to Tralee, where the festival committee undertook to arrange their upkeep in private homes.

'How much more, and how much more loud, can I trumpet the merits of the "Rose of Tralee," that jewel in the crown of the Festival of Kerry?' Terry O'Sullivan asked in Dubliner's Diary. 'Every year here I marvel at just how they can fit one more Rose on the stage.'

In 1972 they managed to fit a total of twenty-nine Roses on stage, new entrants coming from Holland and Switzerland. There was also a Rose from Hawaii for the first time: the wonderfully-named Kathleen Puanani O'Sullivan. She was the great-great-granddaughter of an emigrant from Kerry who arrived in Hawaii on a whaling ship in the middle of the previous century.

'It's four o'clock in the morning, and I have a column to write,' Tom Hennigan wrote in his Going Places column in the *Evening Herald*. 'Not easy to marshal words, clauses, sentences and paragraphs while out there in the street, the evacuation from Dunkirk; and all-Ireland final; a stampede of buffalo, and a Le Mans motor race are all going on at one and the same time.

'This is my first dispatch from the "War of the Roses", here in Tralee. And right now I'm envying the chaps who are quietly and placidly reporting the Vietnam conflict, compared to me, they've a soft job. For the sounds out there defy description. It's a cacophony of incoherent shouts, disjointed snatches of song, demonical laughter; hysterical greetings, and a farewells; slamming of car doors, stuttering engines and tooting horns.'

This page, from top: The Rose from Hawaii, Kathleen Puanani O'Sullivan; The Pelican Steel Band were a new addition. Across: Claire Dubendorfer, Rose of Tralee 1972 with compere Michael Twomey

Of course, such reports were saturated with hyperbole, but they did convey a sense of the emotion. The writers were obviously intoxicated with the atmosphere around them.

New folk groups introduced were Perkonitis, a group from Latvia, and a Bavarian Brass Band, Messelwang. They played in the streets during the day, along with the other bands and Bernard Ferns or 'Fernie', the Punch and Judy man. He was a ventriloquist, novelty magician, balloon modeler and maker of novelty hats. He moved about the streets intriguing children. It was his fourth year at the Festival.

Columnist Terry O'Sullivan had repeatedly been asking when RTÉ would televise 'this most photogenic occasion which seems to cost nobody anything.' RTÉ had made a short black and white film of the 1971 Festival, and had already televised the Castlebar Song Contest. O'Sullivan argued that the Rose of Tralee would be even more suitable for television, because it had so much colour and glamour. Eurotek Ireland, a private company, was enlisted to do a colour documentary of the Festival.

Claire Dubendorfer of Switzerland was the 1972 Rose of Tralee. The London-born daughter of a Dublin mother and Swiss father, she had entered the contest after reading about it in *Die Frau*, a women's weekly magazine.

✢ Claire Dubendorfer of Switzerland was the 1972 Rose of Tralee.

As usual, local people had their own explanation for why she won. Each year people would come up with different reasons, one more far-fetched than another. In Claire Dubendorfer's case it was supposedly because Jack Lynch had asked for her to be picked because Ireland had just voted to join the EEC. The fact that Switzerland had nothing to do with the EEC seemed irrelevant to those people.

'Until you have seen Tralee in the full bloom of the Festival of Kerry, you don't know what the word "festival" means,' Terry O'Sullivan wrote following the press conference announcing the next year's festival lineup. Bord Fáilte estimated that spending topped £1 million in Tralee during the 1972 festival.

✢ BEHIND THE SCENES ✢

The festival committee at one time had sixty-eight voluntary members, with satellite committees in Australia, Britain, Canada, France, Germany, New Zealand, Ireland and the United States. The logistics of the whole thing were phenomenal. Behind the scenes many people provided Trojan service — in stewarding, arranging the streets and town park programmes, as well as looking after the Roses to ensure that nothing untoward happened to them while they were in Tralee. Paddy Mercer was in charge of the stewards, John Kennedy organised programmes for the streets and Town Park, while Helen Brassil and Eleanor Carrick ran the office year round as employees of the festival for over forty years.

Much of the credit for the early success of the festival was owed over the years to a whole range of Kerry people, not just in Kerry but also around the country, and even around the globe— people like Finbar Cox in Limerick, Bart Cronin, Tim Dennehy, Nannette Barrett and Paddy Moriarty in Dublin, Pat Daly and Mary Rose Teehan in Chicago, Dermot Hussey, Tom Kennedy and Carl Sugrue in New York, Kerry Murphy in Sydney, Joe Landers in Boston, and Eoin Kennedy in Toronto. As the North American operations expanded, Harry Milner, a native of Tralee, became the organizer for United States and Canada. There were also other people with no connection with Kerry who provided invaluable help such as Arthur Walls, Martin Dully, Joe Malone, Bobby Howick, Tony Prendergast and Brian Browne, as well as Joe Delaney in Las Vegas.

❦ 1973 ❦

Many of the founding generation had begun to outgrow the Festival of Kerry. Denis J. Reen, a young dentist, was elected as Chairman of the festival committee for 1973. Denis was a brilliant organiser who injected new life into the festival. Richard O'Sullivan, a young veterinary surgeon, was brought on the seven-member board. Many new members were introduced, and a new generation essentially took control. Margaret Dwyer stepped down as President in November 1973, but remained active on the committee as Honorary Secretary.

Brendan O'Reilly of RTÉ was the compere for a second time in 1973.

'What are your ambitions?' he asked Melbourne Rose Annette Mulvihill.

'To marry and have children,' she replied.

'And have you anyone in particular in mind?' he asked 'No.'

While she may not have had at the time, Annette subsequently married and settled in Tralee.

The Swiss Rose had a more novel ambition: to be the first woman on the moon.

The Rose of Tralee for 1973 was Veronica McCambridge of Belfast.

❧ The Rose of Tralee for 1973 was Veronica McCambridge of Belfast

The twenty-seven young women were interviewed under enormous time constraints. Just three minutes were allotted for each interview, as the selection was supposed to be over in a couple of hours.

'Still, there were some annoying lapses,' Christina Murphy noted in *The Irish Times*. Adrian Cronin of RTÉ, who was one of the Rose judges, told the audience that the judges 'were not looking for beauty alone, but were trying to see if they had "a little imagination, intelligence and personality". I'm sure you didn't really mean it, Adrian, but oh, did we females in the audience cringe,' Murphy wrote. But she was effusive about other aspects of the festival.

'It is extraordinary. Try to imagine a medium-sized Irish town rose bedecked and fairy-lit with thousands of people walking about the streets all day and all night long. The pubs are full, of course, but so are the streets. There is a fantastic selection of free street entertainment which ranges over magicians, Josef Locke, Na Fili and the Chieftains. You can buy blankets, transistor radios, footballs, bicycles, hamburgers, crubeens or a new variety of soft drug known as sea grass (dilisk to your grandmother) in stalls along the street.

'I'd been warned about conmanship and over-charging,' she added. 'I wasn't ten minutes in Tralee, when I was disabused of this idea. The taxi man who picked me up (in the most proper sense of the word) at the station asked for 25p fare. He had no change and neither had I. "Sure, leave it," he said, "'tis all in the interest of the Festival" and refused point blank to call back next day for the fare.'

Even the gardai were in good humour in the early hours of the morning.

'Would you move on there, Dennis, and stop giving me grey hairs,' was the typical way in which they cleared the Festival Club at 3 am.

Each year the editors of the Dublin daily newspapers would send down sceptical reporters, who did not expect much, with the result that they were usually pleasantly surprised at what they found. 'I had this idea that I wouldn't like the Festival, after all women editors don't approve of beauty contests and the Rose of Tralee is a beauty queen - isn't she?" Janet Martin of the *Irish Independent* wrote from Tralee during the 1973 festival. 'For me it was the first one and I reckon it will be next five weeks before I catch up on the sleep I have been missing.'

A Bord Fáilte survey of the 1973 festival found that 28,000 people visited Tralee during the week. Young people working in Tralee from other parts of the country inevitably had friends down for the week, and they slept on the floors or in tents in the back gardens of houses throughout the town. Around 69% of the overnight visitors came from other parts of Kerry, 18% from the rest of the Republic, 11% from overseas, and 2% from Northern Ireland. About £700,000 changed hands during the week and between

Across, from top: Veronica McCambridge, Rose of Tralee 1973 with Brendan O'Reilly, Margaret Dwyer and Denis Reen; Roses outside Leinster House. 1973
This page: Roses greet the crowds in the parade

'Below: The Dome; the ad for the Rose of Tralee Massage Parlour'
Across: Margaret Flaherty, Rose of Tralee 1974

£350,000 and £400,000 was generated by the festival, of that £55,000 was spent by tourists from abroad, while Irish residents from outside Kerry spent a further £100,000.

In view of the demand for tickets for the Rose selection, talks were already underway for the festival committee to obtain their own place in which to stage the various events.

❦ 1974 ❦

A huge marquee, covering 18,000 square feet and capable of holding 2,500 people, was purchased for £20,000. Christened The Dome, this would be the home for a number of festival events and also for the Rose selection in 1974. It allowed the festival committee to generate its own capital. Although events on the streets still remained free, admission was charged for the various events held in the Dome.

The float parade generated more interest than ever as a result of competition between the workers of various businesses: the ESB, Gaeltarra Eireann, Ivernia, the Junior Chamber of Commerce, Lions International, Kerry Precision Ball, *The Kerryman* newspaper, Kingdom Tubes, Macra na Feirme, and Traly Footwear. Kerry Precision Ball's entry, Riverboat, was the winner of the £100 prize

A LITTLE BIT OF SCANDAL

In 1974 the festival made the Sunday papers in the tale of an unseemly squabble that was termed the Battle of the Roses. The former organiser in New Zealand claimed that the festival committee was making £1 million a year, and he was suing for £25,000 in the New Zealand courts for alleged 'sharp business practices', because the festival committee had taken the New Zealand franchise from him and given it to a travel company, with the result that he lost business.

Shortly afterwards photographs were sent to Irish newspapers of what purported to be a giant billboard advertising the Rose of Tralee Massage Parlour in New Zealand. It promised an escort service with topless masseuses, and gave a telephone number stipulating that home and hotel calls were a specialty on weekends.

for the best float, with the ESB second, and Traly Footwear third.

The Garda Band, which was on its first visit to Tralee, led off the parade of eleven floats, interspersed with local clubs and other bands, including a visiting US Air Force Band stationed in Germany.

The International Musical Groups contest, which was televised by RTÉ and Dutch TV, involved fifteen groups. The early rounds were contested on a stage in the streets, with the six finalists to appear in the Dome on Thursday night. The proceedings were presented as a one-hour programme on RTE at the end of October.

The Hallmarks, a San Francisco group, won the £1,000 first prize, with the Brannigans of Dublin as runners-up. The whole contest more than paid for itself, because the groups had provided entertainment throughout the week, and the festival charged admission to the Dome for the Grand Final. A variety show was also staged in the Dome, with headliners like Niall Tobin, Joe Cuddy, Josef Locke, Dermot O'Brien and Johnny McEvoy appearing on the one show.

Many of the younger visitors brought tents and camped in the town park until the John Mitchell GAA club opened its football field for camping. The clubhouse had shower and toilet facilities and room for hundreds of tents. Importantly, it could also provide security, ensuring that the tents were safe to leave in place during the day and the occupants were secure at night. This initiative quickly became the club's biggest annual earner, and other clubs in town soon followed suit. This greatly enhanced the town's capacity during the festivities.

🌹 Twenty-year-old Margaret Flaherty, a model from New York, was selected as Rose of Tralee 1974

Some private bus companies, such as Kennedys in Annascaul and Buckleys in Killarney, also ran what amounted to a ferry service into and out of the town each night.

Twenty-year-old Margaret Flaherty, a model from New York, was selected as Rose of Tralee 1974 from twenty-six contestants.

Gay Byrne, the host of the hugely popular and long-running 'Late Late Show', was compere for the first time and he added real professionalism to the contest with his interviewing techniques.

❦ 1975 ❦

The death of former President Eamon de Valera in August 1975 briefly threatened to cancel that year's Festival of Kerry. For many he was seen as one of the country's founding fathers and the virtual personification of an independent Ireland. But he had enjoyed a long life and was well into his nineties when he died, so it was decided to mark his death with a public commemoration, and then continue with the festivities.

The Rose competition was again expanded, with the inclusion of contestants from Galway, Ohio, Pennsylvania, and Peterboro in Ontario, Canada. 'The whole thing was extremely well stage-managed and there was quite an air of pageantry about the proceedings in the Dome,' Christina Murphy noted in *The Irish Times*. The Dome was a sellout on the nights of the Rose selection.

Interviews were conducted 'in a completely unpatronising manner,' Murphy continued. 'The whole proceedings, as much from the girls' input as Mr Byrne's, were most entertaining.'

Above: Maureen Shannon, Rose of Tralee 1975, is congratulated by her fellow Roses
Below: Maureen conducts the Garda Band

The Rose of Tralee that year was Maureen Shannon, a farmer's daughter from Bahola, County Mayo. The London Rose, she had been working in a bank in the English capital for the past three years.

❦ The Rose of Tralee that year was Maureen Shannon

New to the week's activities in 1975 was a fishing competition. A tagged ray was let loose in Tralee Bay, and there was a prize of £1,250 for anyone who could catch it on a rod and line. Dick Sullivan, the President of the festival, had told the summer press conference at Guinness, that 'anybody who attempted to empty Tralee Bay in order to catch the golden tagged ray would be disqualified.' The competition generated a good deal of publicity, but the fish was the fabled 'one that got away' – nobody caught the ray.

The big entertainment attractions were the Army Number One and Number Two bands, which were overshadowed numerically by a US Army Band. The open-air variety shows on the street platforms featured comedian Jack Cruise, singers Frank Patterson, Candy Devine, Tony Kenny, Sandy Shaw of 'Puppet on a String' fame, Cahir O'Doherty, showband stars Big Tom of the Mainliners and Tina of the Nevada, traditional Irish singer Sean Ó Sé with a rousing version of his signature song 'An Poc ar Buille', and, of course, the Wolfe Tones. The prize fund for the entertainment contest was £2,000.

There was an element of organised chaos about the street entertainment. Temporary stages were located in Lower Bridge Street, the Square, the Mall, and the Ashe Memorial Hall, while the steps of the Court House and the front of the Bank of Ireland served as natural bandstands. Adding to the confusion, some of the marching bands would stage impromptu performances in the centre of the streets between the stages.

The Rose contestants would attend various functions early in the week, along with the judges, who watched how they mixed, and how they got on with various people. The judges would then interview each of the Roses separately. This meant that they usually had their minds made up before the formal Rose Selection contest and would merely consult each other after the on-stage interviews to reaffirm their earlier decision, unless their original selection fared very badly in the public interview. This is reputed to have happened at least once during the competition.

❧ 1976 ❧

Shortly before the 1976 festival, the transfer of Bishop Eamonn Casey from Kerry to Galway was announced. At the beginning of the festival week, the Priests' Council sent ballot papers to the clergy in the diocese to indicate their preferences for his replacement. The papers were to be returned within two weeks, but on Friday, the eve of the opening of the festival, the appointment of Dr Kevin McNamara was announced.

'What is annoying is the lack of consultation which we have come to expect from the time of Vatican II,' one prominent cleric told *The Kerryman*. 'What is galling is the decision to overlook the recommendations of Vatican II on the appointment of bishops altogether.'

It was generally felt that the Church had used the festival as camouflage for the timing of the announcement.

The new bishop, a reserved, aloof academic at Maynooth College, was considered the antithesis of the popular, outgoing Bishop of Kerry, who was a larger than life figure.

Gaeltacht Minister Tom O'Donnell opened the festival, which he compared to Mardi Gras with the vitality of its events, music and dancing in the streets. He paid particular tribute to Siamsa Tire, the national folk theatre established in Tralee. The local group was about to tour the US as part of the Irish Government's response to an

Above, from top: The Garda Band on parade; A local priest keeps a fatherly eye on proceedings

🌿 The New York Rose, Marie Soden, twenty-three, a professional model, was chosen as the Rose of Tralee

American invitation to take part in their bicentennial celebrations. The New York Rose, Marie Soden, twenty-three, a professional model, was chosen as the Rose of Tralee. Although born in New York, she grew up in County Cavan and had returned to New York as an eighteen-year-old.

🌿 1977 🌿

Gay Byrne decided to step down as compere in 1977, but the festival committee were anxious to retain their ties with him, so they invited his wife, Kathleen Watkins, to replace him in that year.

There was an extra Rose in 1977: Patty Matyas, whose maternal roots were in Drogheda, represented Las Vegas. This brought the number of participating Roses to 28. The eventual winner was twenty-year-old Orla Burke, a student nurse at Ardkeen Hospital in Waterford. She was the second eldest of a family of twelve children, the youngest of whom was only two at the time.

🌿 The eventual winner was twenty-year-old Orla Burke

There were nearly 1,000 entertainers in Tralee during the week. The entertainment at the Dome included the first live performance in Tralee of the legendary Liam Clancy and Tommy Makem.

Above, from top: Marie Soden, Rose of Tralee 1976 is kissed by her parents; Orla Burke, Rose of Tralee 1977 is congratulated by fellow Roses

Sixteen local groups vied with each other in building the floats. *The Kerryman* won with a large scallop-shell motif, which the staff had been working on since June.

A Dutch group, Kings Galliard, strummed and piped their way to victory in the Folk/Ballad competition, playing a mixture of fiddle, drums, guitar, mandolin, and pipes of pan. Val Joyce of RTÉ hosted the final in the Dome. First prize was £1,000, along with a recording contract with CBS records and a trophy from *Starlight* Magazine. The runners-up were an Australian group, the Bushwackers, whose very distinctive sound was made from beer bottle tops, which they called 'a lager phone'. Quilty, a group from Derry, finished third. The standard was considered very high that year, but the Dome was little more than half-full for the final. There were simply too many attractions elsewhere.

The Festival Club remained particularly popular as an afterhours

Above: Sheila Ann Horgan with Carmel Quinn, on winning the New York heat in 1959
Below: Elizabeth Shovlin, Rose of Tralee 1978

watering hole. On one night in 1976 eleven members of the Kerry football team were counted with drink in hand at 2.30 am. At the time the team was in training for the all-Ireland final. Kerry had unexpectedly beaten the holders Dublin in 1975, but many local people were not surprised when Dublin got their revenge in 1976, although there was no suggestion that it was down to activities in Tralee!

❧ 1978 ❧

Gay Byrne returned as compere of Rose Selection in 1978, and this time the proceedings were televised live. He had persuaded RTÉ to run a three-hour programme, with just a break for the nine o'clock news. It was also at his initiative that the 'talent spot' which has become a staple of the Rose selection, was begun. He and his assistant, Maura Connolly, interviewed the contestants to see who could be invited to perform on stage. On the night, Enda Jackson from Waterford sang, Kate Quirk from Holyoke played the flute, and Cynthia O'Connor from Michigan dedicated 'The Desert Song' to her parents in the audience who were celebrating their 25th wedding anniversary. The *Kerryman* noted that 'Those performance could pack the Dome with their own show'.

Justice Minister Gerard Collins opened the festival. This was followed by a fireworks display with a variety of band recitals at different points in the town at the same time. The Tralee Pipe Band was in Bridge Street, Millstreet Pipe Band on Castle Street, Castlelyons Pipe Band on Rock Street, Cumann Chuculainn Band in St. John's Park and St. David's Pipe Band at Moyderwell Cross. As these were all playing at the same time, within about a half-mile radius of the centre of town, the sound must have been mighty!

The Rose Ball was held on Saturday night, with tickets costing £6.50. The big attractions in the Dome were the Brendan Grace Show on Monday night with Liam Clancy and Tommy Makem following after the Rose Selection on Tuesday, while Bunny Carr's 'Quicksilver' game show was televised from the Dome on Wednesday night. Val Joyce and Mike Murphy presented a final music show comprising selected groups who had been playing on the various stages

❧ Pennsylvania Rose, Elizabeth Shovlin, 20, from Wilkinsburg, was selected as the Rose of Tralee.

around the town all week.

Pennsylvania Rose, Elizabeth Shovlin, 20, from Wilkinsburg, was selected as the Rose of Tralee. The eldest of eight children, both of her parents had emigrated from Donegal in 1957. She was working for a travel agency in East McKeesport, Pennsylvania, and said she hoped to become an airline stewardess, preferably with Aer Lingus. Liz danced a reel on stage.

The television broadcast, for which Gay Byrne received a Jacobs award, was a reminder to viewers watching in Ireland of the many people who had been forced to emigrate. The coverage went down well with most, but not with Ken Gray of *The Irish Times*.

He thought that giving over three hours of prime television time was excessive. 'It was a great self indulgence to let the cameras roll all night,' he wrote, but then went on in a somewhat contradictory manner 'The Rose of Tralee marathon would undoubtedly have lost something if it had been edited down to an hour and transmitted the evening following the event, which would seem to be the logical way to have handled it.'

Editing the programme might have improved it in one sense, but it would have detracted from its spontaneity. Part of the programme's appeal was that anything might happen. Somebody could make a terrible *faux pas*, or simply fall flat on her face.

Gay Byrne felt that the media was hostile to RTÉ. 'Irish newspapers are remarkably selective about what they decide to print or not to print in relation to RTÉ,' he noted in his *Sunday World* column. When RTÉ announced that the Rose Selection programme had attracted a record audience, the press largely ignored the viewing figures.

The ratings indicated that the programme's audience increased each night the longer it went on. This increase was apparent both in the single channel areas, where only RTÉ could be received, and the multi-channel regions, where British channels could also be picked up.

Above, from top: Is that the time? Gay Byrne brought all his Late Late interviewing skills to the Rose stage;
He has his eyes examined by Waterford's medical Rose, Siobhan Kiernan

'I don't know what viewers expected from The Rose of Tralee show,' Gay wrote, 'but there has been only a small number of programmes down through the years which have elicited such a flood of congratulatory and laudatory messages to me personally.'

The feedback in Kerry was that the festival had been the most successful to date. 'The Tralee festival has been twenty years a-growing,' Terry O'Sullivan noted. 'In my job I've attended nineteen

of them. To my mind it is the best of the lot, the most light-hearted and unsophisticated, the most full of laughter and without any evidence of excess.'

While there was no shortage of drinking, there was little violence. There was, however, one tragic, freak accident when a student was killed when he becme impaled on railings at St. John's Parish Church while taking a short cut from the Town Park back to the campsite. Thereafter the gate was left open.

❦ 1979 ❦

In 1979 the pipe bands had competition from an unusual quarter – a couple of West Indian steel bands. The price of tickets for the Rose Ball almost doubled, to £12 each, but there was still no shortage of takers.

The Dome played host to a different late show every night: the Furey Brothers and Davy Arthur on Sunday, the inevitable Wolfe Tones on Monday, with Liam Clancy and Tommy Makem coming on stage following the Rose Selection on Tuesday night. The maximum charge for each of those shows was £4. However, as they could only cater for a couple of thousand people at a time, most of the entertainment remained on the streets or in the pubs.

'The other night when one band failed to turn up on time at the designated location, the organisers rushed in a replacement from further up the street,' Dick Hogan reported in *The Irish Times*. 'One of the Jamaican steel bands in town for the week saw the predicament just before this and came to lend a hand. So did the Garda Band. Then the original band arrived as well. The result was a most glorious confusion of sound which left the thousands on the street rapturous with delight and disbelief and the street entertainment committee with a glint in their eyes. In Tralee, on the run-up to the Rose Selection, they like a bit of well-planned chaos.'

❧ Belfast Rose Marita Marron, a civil servant from Andersontown, was named Rose of Tralee.

Above, from top: A youngster gets into the festival mood
Marita Marron, Rose of Tralee 1979, waves to the crowd

Belfast Rose Marita Marron, a civil servant from Andersontown, was named Rose of Tralee. She was frank about her home town in her televised interview. 'It is not a very nice place to live,' she told Gay Byrne, 'and it is not a great place to bring up a family.' Normally anyone knocking their place of birth like that would have turned off the judges, but in the midst of the Northern troubles, everyone could understand her attitude.

But the interview that attracted most attention was with the Cailín Gaelach, Moire Ní Cheide, who was very entertaining about Irish curse words and playing Gaelic football. Gay Byrne was so impressed by this zany interview that he actually had her as a guest on the 'Late Late Show' some weeks later.

❦ THE EIGHTIES ❦

In 1980 Charles Haughey met the Roses at Leinster House. 'The Taoiseach could charm the petals off a rose,' wrote Isobel Conway of the *Irish Press*.

Haughey warmly greeted the Roses and even invited them to Inishvickallane, his island off the Kerry coast. 'Be careful of those Kerrymen,' he warned. 'Many a beautiful lady before you has gone down to Kerry and never come back again.'

Catherine Farnan, the Pennsylvania Rose, presented the Taoiseach with an American football from the Superbowl winning team, the Pittsburg Steelers.

Tom McEllistrim, jr., a Minister of State and local Dáil deputy, opened the festival. The usual bands were playing throughout the town, and the Rose Ball was held on Saturday night for the last time. Henceforth it would be held on Friday, because it was not possible to secure a legal exemption for the bars to remain open past midnight. One local Garda sergeant felt that nobody should be above the law. He famously raided the annual Garda social one night and closed it down. Shortly after his appointment, as Minister, McEllistrim was performing the ceremonial opening of a building, an enterprising photographer recorded the scene with the garda sergeant in the background giving a ticket to the illegally parked state car! The sergeant arrived at the door of the Rose Ball on more than one occasion on which the Minister for Justice was enjoying the festivities inside. John Doyle, the Chief Superintendent, had to order him not to raid the Dome. After the second time the Chief Superintendent quietly requested the festival committee to move the Rose Ball to Friday night.

The late night concerts in the Dome in 1980 included Johnny Logan, twice winner of the Eurovision Song Contest, the Chieftains, Joe Dolan, festival regulars Liam Clancy and Tommy Makem, and the Wolfe Tones.

One of the talking points of the 1980 Rose selection was the

Above, from top: Roses on LE Orla, 1996;
Sheila Hanrahan, Rose of Tralee 1980

second appearance of Adele Hanafin of Melbourne. She had represented the city four years earlier. 'The whole thing arose out of the change of committee in Melbourne and we didn't cop on to the fact that it was the same girl until we saw her,' festival President Joe Murphy explained. Nowdays the eligibility rules preclude anyone who has previously competed.

❧ At the age of twenty-six, Sheila O'Hanrahan from Galway became the oldest Rose of Tralee

At the age of twenty-six, Sheila O'Hanrahan from Galway became the oldest Rose of Tralee since the competition began. She was a social worker with the Western Health Board. Although Sheila was born in Dublin she was from Roscommon, where her father was County Surgeon for many years. 'Sheila was born in Dublin because there was no proper maternity unit in Roscommon at that time,' local politician Terry Leyden complained. 'We still haven't got one.'

Fergus Pyle, the former editor of *The Irish Times* was unimpressed with the televised Rose Selection. 'RTÉ should be able to provide better than what was, in effect, parish-hall fun,' Pyle complained.

Below: Debbie Carey, Rose of Tralee 1981

❧ 1981 ❧

While at first the nightly concerts had been a novelty, year after year they were losing their appeal. In 1981 the festival committee came up with the idea of replacing the concerts with the Festival Club in the Dome. This proved particularly successful for a number of years, although the free drink had long been done away with at this stage.

Birmingham Rose, Deborah Carey, 21, became the first Rose of Tralee from Britain since 1967. Her Irish cousins from Buncrana, County Donegal were in the audience. At the time she was engaged to Hibernian soccer player, Ian Henry.

Yet again, *The Irish Times* was not amused. Niall Fallon asked, 'is it not odd that women who seek to be equal to men should by taking part in the degrading charade of the Rose of Tralee contest, make nonsense of their own pleas to be taken seriously?'

❧ Birmingham Rose, Deborah Carey, 21, became the first Rose of Tralee from Britain since 1967.

IN GUILT AND GLORY

David Hanly — later presenter of RTÉ's popular current affairs programme, 'Morning Ireland' — parodied the Rose of Tralee in his 1979 novel, In Guilt and In Glory. It featured a Cahirciveen Carrot Queen Festival, the judges of which based their choice on 'uprightness, intelligence and personality', according to Hanly, 'for the virtues of a good Carrot Queen were those not of the professional beauty, but of the good housewife'. The winner was awarded 'the Golden Carrot'.

The book was apparently based largely on Hanly's experiences working for Bord Failte. In his book Hanly also had a woman character with a Brooklyn accent as president of the Caherciveen Carrot Queen Festival. She was described as 'a third generation returned Yank named Mrs. Amelia Line, known to locals as the Widdah Line.'

In later years, there was the 'Lovely Girls' competition on TV's 'Father Ted'. These parodies were a measure of how the Rose of Tralee had established itself and become such a recognisable feature of Irish culture.

The subsequent Tam ratings estimated that 543,000 households were tuned into the programme, well in excess of the second-ranked programme, 'Flamingo Road', which had 409,000, while the second highest rated home-produced programme had 374,000. The highest rating any programme got during Pope John Paul's visit to Ireland the previous September was 488,000.

Those figures did not invalidate the views of either Pyle or Fallon, which were espressed as opinion columnists. Notwithstanding, the show continued to attract a massive viewing audience, which suggests that Pyle and Fallon were out of touch with a huge proportion of the country.

❧ 1982 ❧

Taoiseach Charles J. Haughey again met the Roses for a photo, thereby provided great publicity for the festival.

In its third decade, the Festival of Kerry had become a major television event. The bright lights and the noise in the streets were still going on, but the festival moved into a different gear on television. The Rose selection in the Dome was extended to two nights, with RTÉ covering both nights live on television.

Although the Festival Club had replaced many of the nightly concerts, the Wolfe Tones returned for a concert in 1982 and an outside promoter put on a one night extravaganza with some of the biggest Irish names in folk music: Freddie White, Christy Moore, The Dubliners, Stockton's Wing, and Folkstone.

Laura Gainey, 22, of Peterborough, Ontario, became the first Canadian to be selected Rose of Tralee. She was a student of public administration who hoped to go on to Law School. Again the television ratings were high despite some carping among the critics.

Left: Laura Gainey (wearing the Peterborough sash) is announced as Rose of Tralee 1982
Across: Brenda Hyland, Rose of Tralee 1983

🌿 Laura Gainey, 22, of Peterborough, Ontario, became the first Canadian to be selected Rose of Tralee.

Over the years the festival committee was particularly anxious that none of the Roses should be photographed with a glass of stout. This was not out of any sense of prudishness, but simply to prevent any suggestion that the young women were being exploited by the main sponsors of the festival.

In *Image* magazine in March 1982, former Rose of Tralee Marie Soden was quoted as having said that Guinness was a 'healthy drink', and that she drank it in New York when she was 17 years old. The article libellously asserted that, when she was not working or at dinner parties, she could be seen drinking Guinness at her favourite bar.

Marie denied ever making any of those statements. They were pure inventions, she said. She was paid £100 for the interview, but she declined the cheque from *Image*. She had understood that the subject was to be her personal life as a model, Rose of Tralee and an amateur pilot. What appeared, however, was substantially about Guinness and was, in fact, an endorsement of the drink.

'What could be more defamatory of any young or old, single or married woman than to portray her as sitting up drinking at a bar in this fashion? Who would like to think of their daughter or wife, mother or grandmother doing this?' Judge Frank Roe asked. 'Who would want their son to be seen with a girl like that?' He awarded Marie Soden £2,000 in damages and ruled that Guinness brewery should pay the damages and costs in the case.

🌿 1983 🌿

Initially the big talking point of 1983 festival was the appearance of James Last and his orchestra at the Austin Stack Park on the Sunday. This was televised live on RTÉ in front of a crowd of around 12,000. That year's festival also marked the extension of the race meeting to five days. Rose Selection went well on both nights and the ultimate winner of Rose of Tralee was Brenda Hyland of Waterford, a trainee at the Garda College in Templemore. This went down particularly well on the night, as the Garda Band was playing for the occasion.

🌿 The winner of Rose of Tralee was Brenda Hyland, a trainee garda

But outside the Dome storm clouds were gathering as Hurricane Charlie made its way to Ireland. Plans had been made to televise 'Trom agus Eadrom', the popular bilingual variety show hosted by Liam Ó Murchu from the Dome on the Thursday evening, but as the winds mounted during the afternoon, it was decided to cancel that night's programme. Fortunately, the Dome was empty and most of the television equipment was had been removed before the Dome came crashing down that evening.

This page, from top: The Dome was flattened by Hurricane Charlie in 1983; All the Roses at the Earl of Desmond hotel. Diane Hannagan (standing, right) became Rose of Tralee 1984 Across: The massive Wolfe Tone audience; Helena Rafferty, Rose of Tralee 1985 is overcome att her selection

Diane was chosen as the new Rose of Tralee

❦ 1984 ❦

One feature of the 1984 festival was the opening of a new, bigger and more modern Dome. Michael McNulty, the Director General of Bord Failte, officially opened the festival with the usual line up of bands, along with the New York City Police Pipe Band. Two steel bands — Pelican and Marco Petrassi — circulated around the town on the back of a truck.

Dick Spring was in the front row at Rose Selection, and Gay Byrne raised some eyebrows when he noted that some people thought 'dick spring' was a kind of sex aid. Cork Rose Noelle Morrison said that Charlie Haughey was the greatest political rogue in history, while Limerick Rose Diane Hannagan listed Mahatma Gandhi as the greatest leader in history. Diane was a student of public administration at the National Institute of Higher Education in Limerick. At the end of the selection process Diane was chosen as the new Rose of Tralee.

❦ 1985 ❦

The Wolfe Tones were the big attraction in Tralee in 1985. It was twenty-one years since they first made their name in Tralee, and they played an open-air concert after the new Rose of Tralee was presented to the crowd on the platform at the Ashe Memorial Hall. A massive audience, estimated at over 30,000, turned up for the free concert and many people had to be treated when they were overcome in the crush in the confines of the railings of the Town Park at the lower end of Denny Street. Fortunately nobody was seriously injured.

The line up for the street entertainment included six pipe bands, the Band of the Southern Command, the Pelican Steel Band, the Leeside Jazz Band, Loc Gormain Silver Band, Tallaght Community Youth Band, and two rock groups, RPM and Ace. All played at various locations around the town immediately after the official opening. They continued to play in the streets throughout the week, along with the Dublin City Ramblers and a Bavarian folk group. There were also appearances by comedians Cha and Miah, and Brendan Grace.

That festival marked a return to early evening concerts, this time in the new Dome, followed by a late night cabaret in the Festival Club each night. The early shows consisted of Christy Moore on Saturday, Phil Coulter on Sunday and Joe Dolan on Monday. Among the peripheral events were golf competitions throughout the week, the traditional Track and Field meeting at St John's Athletic Club, the Greyhound racing at the Dog Track, and the Dog Show, but, like the horse racing, these were all run independently of the festival itself, though the Rose of Tralee would usually present some of the prizes.

Helena Rafferty, 18, of Boston was selected Rose of Tralee. She had an unusual talent — sign language — and had Gay Byrne sing 'The Rose of Tralee' while she signed the words. She was the first Boston winner in twenty-two years.

❦ Helena Rafferty, 18, of Boston was selected Rose of Tralee.

❦ 1986 ❦

James Last returned to the Austin Stack Park for another open air concert on Saturday evening just before Dick Spring formally

opened the 1986 festival. Kerry were playing Meath in the all-Ireland senior football semi-final the following day, so Kerry Group erected a big screen in the Town Park as part of its annual spectacular. The Kerry team duly won, much to the delight of the bulk of the gathering.

Noreen Cassidy of Leeds was selected as the Rose of Tralee. A student of politics, she told Gay Byrne that politicians were good actors. 'Sorry, Dick,' she then added, turning to Dick Spring in the front row. Her father, Patrick, was from Williamstown, County Galway.

Noreen Cassidy of Leeds was selected as the Rose of Tralee

'Like all the best politicians, Noreen was well prepared for the surprise outcome on Wednesday night,' Brenda Power noted in the *Irish Press*. 'Back stage, after the results were announced, she faced the press with a speech and a delivery that could have been stage-managed by Margaret Thatcher's image makers.'

The Festival of Kerry, like the whole country, was in financial trouble during the mid 1980s. In 1986 Denis Reen was again persuaded to bring his organisational talents to the rescue. He had slipped out of the festival in the late 1970s to become involved in other matters, including the creation of a world class golf links at the relocated Tralee Golf Club and the establishment of Na Gaedheal GAA club. By the latter part of the 1980s Denis was turning his hand to a new project — the construction of the Aqua Dome in Tralee. Of course, there were many other people involved, but he was the driving inspiration in the voluntary effort to secure the necessary investment in the various projects.

1987

Charles J. Haughey returned to power in 1987 and he journeyed to Tralee to open the festival. As befitted a patron of the arts, he did it in verse:

'When I return to Kerry
Like a Roman back to Rome
I always get that feeling
Of a man who's coming home.
When I begin to wonder at what Kerry means to me

I can share with you the magic of the mountains and the sea.
A county packed with stories told beside a heartening fire.
Town and villagers rejoicing at the sight of Sam Maguire …'

Turning to the Roses, he intoned:

'I welcome now the Roses who have come from near and far
From this bright glittering firmament we will chose a single star.
The chosen Rose of '87, queen of land and sea,
The best on earth, a breath of heaven, the new Rose of Tralee,
And though the victory rest with one, my praise goes out to all
The shining girls and Kerry folk, who make this festival.'

Ireland was blighted by a renewed surge of emigration in the 1980s, with much of the younger generation being compelled to leave the country in search of employment. This made Irish people all the more conscious of the Irish Diaspora, and the Rose of Tralee was unquestionably the biggest celebration of that Diaspora as it brought young women of Irish extraction together. The television audience liked to see what was happening to the various generations with Irish connections coming from all over the world. Some were the children or grandchildren of Irish people, but the Irish connections went back much further for others. The magic ingredient was the affinity they retained with Ireland even though their assimilation into other cultures may have been patently apparent.

Gay Byrne was amused at the Belgian Rose, Patricia Sicora, who was a native Flemish speaker. However, her grandmother was from Lurgan, County Down, and she taught Patricia to speak English, which she spoke with a distinct North of Ireland accent. Patricia told of how she learned of her selection to represent Belgium.

'I was with me mammy and me daddy and we were chattin' away, so I didn't hear me name when they announced the winner,' she said. 'Next thing me granny hits me a duff and nearly knocks me off the chair to tell me I'd won.'

Patricia, a student, said that she was 'studying severe'.

'What's "severe", Patricia?' asked a puzzled Gay.

'Somebody who measures land,' she explained. She clearly meant 'surveyor' but pronounced it in the way her Lurgan granny would

Across, from top: Roses at RTE with Gerry Ryan and Dave Fanning; Noreen Cassidy, Rose of Tralee 1986, gasps at the announcement
Above: Charlie Haughey waxes lyrical
Below: Gay has heard enough!

have. The interview was a graphic reminder that ties with Ireland still had an influence on descendants who grew up on the Continent.

Gay asked Patricia about her escort.

'Well, he's alright,' she replied, 'but he's a bit wee.'

The interview went down a treat because it graphically demonstrated the living link with Ireland even after a couple of generations.

Gay was always particularly conscious that most of the young women had never been interviewed on television before and, as the father of two daughters, he went out of his way to ensure that they were not embarrassed or made to look foolish. He skilfully allowed himself to become the butt of their humour, and this went down well with the audience.

He asked the Toronto Rose, Mary O'Connor, whose father came from Killarney, what she was studying.

'Accountancy,' she replied.

Not long before this Gay had lost most of his savings through the activities of his accountant, a fact that was widely known.

'The less said about accountants the better,' Gay rejoined. Most of the audience knew instantly what he was getting at.

Gay remarked that Regina Hoare, the Melbourne Rose, had 'an unfortunate name.'

'We both have unusual names, don't we, Gay?' she countered.

At a rehearsal in the afternoon the girls would perform their planned party pieces. If Gay thought they would look foolish doing something, he would simply terminate the interview that evening without asking them to perform.

Nora Sheehy was the hot favourite with the betting public. Her mother had been the Carnival Queen in 1957, while one of her paternal aunts had been the Carnival Queen the following year, and another aunt represented Tralee in the first Rose of Tralee contest in 1959.

However, it was Larna Canoy of Chicago who took the honours as the 1987 Rose of Tralee. Her parents came from St. Louis, but her grandparents were

❧ Larna Canoy of Chicago took the honours as the 1987 Rose of Tralee

from County Clare. She promptly announced that she was giving the £2,000 prize to a charity for children, to be decided by the festival committee.

❦ 1988 ❦

The fact that the festival was still largely run by volunteers was somewhat of a marvel. There had been a number of paid general secretaries, starting with Jim Casey, who was followed by Ted Keane, who retained his ties with the festival on a voluntary basis after he went to work for Burlington Industries in the late 1980s. Paddy Drummond then took up the position after he retired from the Electricity Supply Board.

'Since I have been associated with the festival over the past ten years I have never failed to be amazed at the way it is run,' Gay Byrne told journalists.

'The festival is run with military precision by an enthusiastic army of volunteers willing to go through endless hours without sleep to ensure that everything runs according to schedule,' Dick Hogan noted in *The Irish Times*.

Charles Haughey opened the festival again in 1988, and had another ditty for the occasion. His opening line, 'People triumph when they believe they can' predated by twenty years Barack Obama's famous rallying cry, 'Yes, we can'.

People triumph when they believe they can
Therefore I say to you tonight,
'Come celebrate with me,
Come celebrate the Kingdom of delight.

When I salute this hosting of my friends,
and welcome visitors from near and far
And welcome heartily the smiling Roses,
Each rose, a fair, particular star.

People of Kerry, Roses, visitors,

Across, from top: The Belfast Rose has some fun with her escort; Gay with Cork Rose Kay Cosgrave
Above: Larna Canoy, Rose of Tralee 1987
Below: A road sweeper gets the brush-off from the London and Kerry Roses

Let everyone man, woman, girl, and boy
Proclaim that once again this Kingdom's capital
Is the capital of joy.'

'The Roses evoke quite a different stereotype of womanhood,' columnist and later author Nuala O' Faolain noted. 'To me, the most sweet and moving thing about the whole competition is the shots of the parents in the audience, absolutely choking with pride in their daughters.'

Nuala's father, Terry O'Sullivan, the columnist and one of the first judges of the Rose of Tralee, had apparently infused her with some of his own enthusiasm for the festival.

'The Rose of Tralee has taken the cruel, vacuous form of the beauty contest, and infused it with other values,' she wrote. 'Not radically, not departing altogether from its source, but molding it to be about the family, not the individual and about place, real place, not the limboland of television.

'You find yourself wishing those lovely girls well and hoping they'll be lucky and happy always. This is the opposite of voyeurism. That an interaction so human could arise from a popularity contest says a lot for the organisers, for the television producer, and a lot for a society still warmly clinging to the village and all it stands for.'

Roses who scored off Gay Byrne went down particularly well with the audience. When he asked Maryanne Murphy of New Zealand if she had a boy back home, she responded 'I have a *man* back home in New Zealand.'

Maryanne, whose grandparents came from Killarney, was chosen as the Rose of Tralee that year. She was a hotel receptionist in her native Invercargill.

Carmel Mulhern, 19, of Brisbane had been the bookies fancy after the first night. Gay said he always got the decision wrong. He would have chosen the girl with the golden voice from South Wales, Karen Carr. According to Gay, even the escorts got it wrong: 'Maryanne was popular, of course, but they didn't back her with hard cash.'

However, he felt 1988 wasn't 'as memorable as, say last year when the Belgium girl, Patricia Sicora, made everyone laugh,' he said. 'That's what I miss most, a good laugh and someone a little off the wall. I feel the judges are inclined to choose more

Maryanne Murphy, whose grandparents came from Killarney, was chosen as the Rose of Tralee

Across: Maryanne Murphy with Hazel Hawke, wife of the Prime Minister of Australia, Bob Hawke
Below: Gay wipes a tear from the face of Maryanne Murphy, Rose of Tralee 1988
Bottom: Boyzone and Roses

conservative girls nowadays.'

Financially, the festival was doing well. The Rose Ball, the two nights of Rose Selection and six nights of the Festival Club were generally sell-outs, with the result that the Dome income was £124,575 for the week. This amounted to a clear profit of £31,691, and the festival committee also got an extra £113,749 in sponsorship.

It was not only generating valuable publicity for Ireland abroad, but also attracting visitors. The six Australian centres sent 313 people to Tralee and they spent 22 days each in Ireland. A further 25 came from New Zealand, and the American centres sent a total of 1,005 people, while Canada sent 80, Germany and Belgium sent a total of 107, and a further 1,170 came from Britain and the Channel Islands. Nearly all of those people travelled around Ireland, so they were a distinct boost for Irish tourism.

❦ 1989 ❦

The number of Roses from continental Europe doubled from two to four in 1989, with Switzerland and France joining Belgium and Germany. 'They appeared like tinkling shining satellites beamed back to us from the immigrant trail,' Caroline Walsh wrote.

Moya Graf from Nurnberg was sent by her parents to school at Kylemore Abbey for seven years so that she could get an Irish education. She told the audience about her Irish grandmother, Anne Agnew from Cobh. The mother of Vreni Bleiker from Zurich, came from Ballina, while the mother of Tara de Coninck of Belgium came from Inchicore, and Camille Duconte's mother came from Cork.

The attendance at the Rose Selection included the Australian Ambassador Brian Burke, German Ambassador Helmut Rurdreigal and Canadian Ambassador Richard Roberts.

The eventual winner was Sinead Boyle from Dublin. There were over 100,000 on the streets to witness the new Rose of Tralee and the fireworks display, according to the *Irish Press*.

Financially, the festival made a profit of £51,121 and reduced its ongoing debt by 32% to £24,234.

❧ **The eventual winner was Sinead Boyle**

❧ THE NINETIES ❧

❧ 1990 ❧

New York-born Julia Dawson, 23, was selected as the 1990 Rose of Tralee. She was representing Germany where she was a student of design and communications. Julia had been raised near Ennis, County Clare, where her father, Ted, was a farmer. He and her German mother, Hannelore, were in the audience, along with her brother Brian, who had flown over fom New York for the occasion.

Arguably, French Rose Sophie Baumann was the one who stole the show with one of the most memorable interviews of the night. Her difficulties in expressing herself fluently in English were compensated for by her vivid facial expressions and body language. She explained to Gay that she did not like men 'pawing' at her! For her finale she persuaded Gay to do the can-can with her, which went down a storm with the audience.

❧ 1991 ❧

In 1991 Tralee Urban District Council decided to restrict casual traders on the streets during the festivities. The council essentially corralled the traders at the lower end of Abbey Street Car Park for the duration of the festival. Garda Superintendent Fred Garvey had complained that the street traders were getting out of hand. 'Something had to be done because it was attracting a criminal

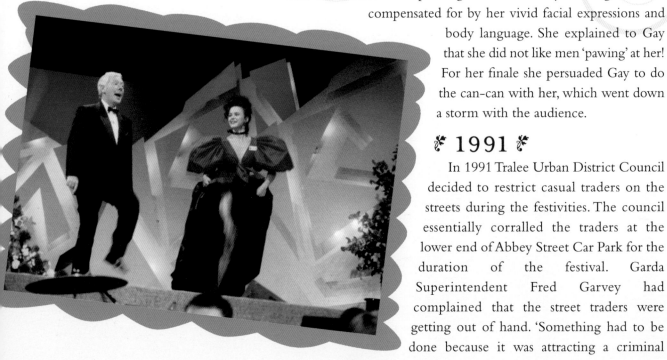

❧ New York-born Julia Dawson, 23, was selected as the 1990 Rose of Tralee

Across, from top: Sinead Boyle, Rose of Tralee 1989; French Rose Sophie Baumann shows Gay how to do the can-can
Above: Julia Dawson, Rose of Tralee 1990

element into the town,' he said. 'Pickpockets were having a field day in the crowds as they stopped at the street vendors, so it was thought that this would control the situation.'

A group of traders appealed to the High Court that they had been trading in the area for up to thirty years, but they were unsuccessful.

Taoiseach Charles Haughey was back to open the festival for his last time in 1991. The political storm clouds were already gathering over his head, but he was in an expansive mood. 'This is a magical Kerry evening,' he said. 'Let there be music, singing and dancing, let there be laughter and joy, let there be fun and happiness for the duration of the festivities.'

He went on to wax lyrical about the original Rose of Tralee, Mary O'Connor, in a verse that contained the immortal lines:

'Born in Brogue Lane, beautiful child of the poor,
Flowing dark hair, the most shining true eyes you could see ...'

After the formal opening he visited the new Geraldine Medieval Experience in the museum at the Ashe Memorial Hall. The museum was another step in the development of Tralee's tourist potential, which had long been one of the prime aims of the festival. Haughey wrote in the visitor's book that the Geraldine Experience was 'an outstanding concept, brilliantly conceived and imaginatively implemented.'

Cork Rose Denise Murphy, 21, was selected as Rose of Tralee from among thirty-two contestants. From the Blackrock area of the city, she worked at Cork airport. She was engaged to be married, and she told Gay Byrne that she wished to honeymoon in Iceland 'because of the twenty hours of darkness'.

Denise made a big impression on stage when, a la Buck's Fizz, she whipped off part of her long ballgown to reveal a short skirt that was more suitable for the Irish dance that she then performed. In the audience were all of Denise's immediate family, along with three

of her grandparents, her fiancé, Thomas O'Sullivan, and Denis Cregan, Lord Mayor of Cork.

When being interviewed in advance by Maura Connolly, Denise mentioned that one of the escorts was particularly funny. As Gay was always on the lookout for some novel twist in the show, he invited the escort, Alan Shortt, on stage, and Shortt used it a the launching pad for his career as a comedian.

Cork Rose Denise Murphy, 21, was selected as Rose of Tralee

Although there were the usual number of bands and singing groups, the removal of the traders from the streets, especially the chip vans, seemed to detract from the festivities. The streets lacked atmosphere, according to Paulette O'Connor of the *Irish Press*. One local councillor slammed the decision to remove the street traders as 'the single most destructive decision in the festival's history'.

One trader said he sold just £6 worth of tee shirts in the car park. 'I come here every year from Waterford and usually make around £150 a day, but this year sales have just been pathetic. One day I didn't even sell anything.'

Above: Denise Murphy, Rose of Tralee 1991 whipped off her long skirt to reveal her Cork City allegiance
Below: Charlie had already picked the winner!

❧ 1992 ❧

The subdued atmosphere was probably reflected the following year by a distinct drop in the crowds, but the festival was still expanding in other ways, with Sunday racing at Ballybeggan Park introduced for the first time. Another first was a Rose from New Orleans, Jennifer Coleman. The influence enjoyed by the festival became apparent when the San Francisco Rose, Noreen McGee, was struck down by gastroenteritis after her arrival in Dublin. She was so ill she decided to go home. Trans World Airways, Aer Lingus, the United States Embassy and the Department of Foreign Affairs all combined to fly over a replacement at the shortest notice. Jennifer Doyle Lopez did not have a passport but the official hurdles were circumvented; she was given an emergency passport to get to Tralee, and she then got a proper passport from the American Embassy in Dublin.

Taoiseach Albert Reynolds was among the 1,100 people who attended the Rose Ball. The Australian Ambassador was also present. Next night the Taoiseach formally opened the festival following the parade, which featured the Roses on thirteen floats, with twelve different bands providing the music.

The Town Park Extravaganza, towards which Kerry Group contributed £40,000 in sponsorship, was a mammoth affair. In addition to the Roses, floats and marching bands, the famous Australian Rolf Harris performed on stage. The Furey Brothers and Jim McCann also featured.

The Furey Brothers had become internationally famous since they first appeared at the Festival a quarter of a century earlier. Finbar Furey recalled their initial visit to the festival in 1966, when their father, Teddy, kept a paternal eye on Eddie, Paul and Finbar. They stayed in one of the horse-drawn caravans provided by the festival committee. They had mighty craic and won first prize. 'Our prize money was £175, which we thought was a fortune. We bought a drink for everybody who took part and the cost of that came to £47.'

Tralee-man Francie Conway, who was making a reputation for himself as a musician, played on the keyboard with the Furey Brothers during their engagement.

The Rose Selection was still considered magnificent television and commanded the highest advertising rates, similar to the 'Late Late Show'. However, Eanna Brophy of the *Sunday Press* thought the 1992 contest betrayed a degree of over-rehearsal on the part of Gay Byrne and the contestants.

'...this year it seemed to me he was left unsurprised by anything they told him ... much of the spontaneity seems to have been taken out.'

'But,' Brophy continued, 'this is judging the event by its own high standards. It still stands head and shoulders above any mere beauty

Top: 'Tie Me Kangaroo Down' Rolf Harris entertains the crowd
Bottom: Some fancy footwork from Albert Reynolds with Catherine McCarthy and Mary Anne Connaughton

contest — because of course it's much more than that.'

The selection programme was running late and the photographer for the *Irish Independent* got some frantic calls from head office to get a photograph of the new Rose of Tralee as soon as possible. They were holding the front page for the picture.

The selection of the Galway Rose, Niamh Grogan, 24, a native of Tullow, County Carlow, as Rose of Tralee went down particularly well with the sixty members of the staff of Channelle, in Loughrea, County Galway, where Niamh worked as a veterinary nurse.

As the press gathered to take the traditional photograph, there was considerable excitement and somebody suggested that, as the new Rose's grandmother was in the audience, she should come up on stage. This, of course, delayed proceedings further and the Independent's photographer was becoming almost hysterical.

'Smile, Granny!' he shouted when they were finally ready. 'Smile, Granny!' he repeated in exasperation. 'For ★★★★'s sake, smile!'

Nobody seemed to notice whether Granny smiled or not, but his colleagues cracked up.

An episode of the popular TV series 'The Big Top' was recorded in the Dome on the last night of the

❧ The selection of the Galway Rose, Niamh Grogan, 24, a native of Tullow, County Carlow, as Rose of Tralee went down particularly well

festival. Other programmes in that series had been filmed in Fossett's circus tent, which held about 700 people, but with the attraction of stars like Daniel O'Donnell, Bagatelle, and Eurovision winners Linda Martin and Johnny Logan, they needed the festival Dome with its much greater capacity.

❦ 1993 ❦

Albert Reynolds was back in Tralee for the festival in 1993, but now he was in coalition with the Labour Party, headed by Dick Spring, who was not about to allow the Taoiseach, or any other member of the government, to upstage him in his hometown. As both Tanaiste and Minister for Foreign Affairs, Spring had met the Roses on Thursday morning at Iveagh House, and he also officially opened the festival.

Albert still made the news, however, when Kirsty Flynn of Midlands, UK, was selected Rose of Tralee. Kirsty, a 23-year-old languages graduate from Southampton University, had worked as a translator with the Miss World pageant in South Africa. She then worked in Brazil for three months before trying her hand at the Rose of Tralee.

❧ Kirsty Flynn of Midlands, UK, was selected Rose of Tralee.

Both of her parents were from Longford, which was part of Reynolds' constituency. 'It's a great day for Longford,' he said as he congratulated Kirsty. He had a particularly good day in picking winners at the races, and he said he had a bet on the winning Rose, too.

'I had a little wager on her but I got bad odds,' he told Pascal Sheehy of *The Kerryman*. He bet on her at 4 to 1. 'All you Kerry people took the good odds.' Backed from 12 to 1 down to 2 to 1, she was the first bookies favourite to win in years.

'Whether it is a good or a bad year for tourism, Kerry always

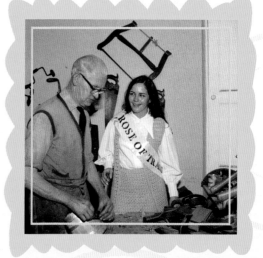

Above: Limerick Rose Paula Flynn waves to the crowd from a futuristic-looking float

Across, from top: Muirne Hurley, Rose of Tralee 1994, shows off her talent on the harp, but it was her father (middle pic) who got to serenade his daughter from the audience

Bottom: Roses meet the local clergy.

seems to be able to get them in,' Reynolds told the press. 'The Rose Festival is a great week in the calendar and it is fantastic to be able to sustain it over 35 years.'

❧ 1994 ❧

In 1992 Gay Byrne had announced that the 1993 festival would certainly be his last. 'I am still at the same stage,' he said in 1993. 'I keep on thinking about it. One of these years I will do it.'

The festival had enormous competition in 1994 with the all-Ireland football semi-final between Dublin and Derry in Croke Park, a rock concert in Cork featuring U2, international show jumping in Millstreet, and the Dingle Regatta.

Ursula Carolyn, the Darwin Rose, had a Malaysian father, but she was very much overshadowed by the Rose from France, Evelyn Faye, 19, of Viroflay, the first black Rose, whose hair was worn in dreadlocks. Her mother was from Dublin and her father from Senegal. One of her brothers was attending Portobello College in Dublin, and he persuaded Evelyn to enter the Rose of Tralee. After a photograph of her holding a glass of beer was published in a newspaper, Dr Mick Loftus, a former President of the GAA, denounced the festival for excessive drinking, even though he had not been to it.

Limerick Rose Muirne Hurley mentioned on stage that her

Kerry-born father, Cormac, a garda in Limerick, had a good singing voice. So instead of asking her to do a party piece, Gay prevailed upon her father in the audience to get up and sing. Dad then serenaded her with 'The Rose of Tralee'. It was no great surprise later that evening when Muirne was selected as the 1994 Rose of Tralee.

The Washington Rose caused some controversy when she recounted the story of two cousins being raped and thrown off a bridge in the United States. Her brother jumped seventy feet from the bridge in an unsuccessful bid to save them, and he had the added horror of being briefly arrested on suspicion of implication in their murder. The audience listened intently.

Muirne was selected as the 1994 Rose of Tralee

'See,' said Gay, 'I told you they would want to hear about it.' But it was too much for some members of the press. In his television review in *The Irish Times* Tom Humphries stated that ' No youngster should have been encouraged to retail such a grim, starkly upsetting story for public consumption like that.'

Actress Jeananne Crowley, on the other hand, was greatly moved by 'the common decency and pride of the parents, their obvious delight in their daughters and the lengths they have come to celebrate their Irishness.' She wrote to *The Irish Times* that Gay Byrne 'was quite right, in my opinion, to encourage the Washington Rose to tell the story of her family's triumph over the kind of nightmare you wouldn't wish on your worst enemy.'

Following the official closing ceremony that year an intoxicated youngster stripped naked and climbed up on the shoulders of the Croppy Boy statue in Denny Street. A large crowd gathered, and cheered as he urinated from the statue. Some irresponsible elements urged him to jump, which would undoubtedly have led to serious injury. Fortunately he was persuaded to come down. As he already had a string of criminal convictions, he was sentenced to a year in jail for his antics — for pissing off the Croppy Boy!

❧ 1995 ❧

Above: Evelyn Faye, the French Rose, enjoys the Kerry scenery Across: Nyomi Horgan, Rose of Tralee 1995 at the races

Ventures Consultancy, a British firm, was hired take a close look at the 1994 festival with the aim of drawing up a £25,000 plan for the future. 'Very little is known factually about the Rose of Tralee Festival,' Ken Robinson, the managing director of the company, explained. 'We need to find out who is coming to Tralee.'

A major survey was conducted with the help of Dr Gearoid O'Donoghue of Tralee Regional College. It found that most visitors came for the entertainment in the pubs and on the streets. Some 43% said that they came primarily for the pub entertainment and 33% for the street entertainment, while 9.8% came for the Rose Selection and just 3.6% for the Rose Ball. The numbers who came for the dress events was comparatively small, even though those got most publicity.

'On the street a different festival is taking place,' Dick Hogan of *The Irish Times* noted. 'The pubs are standing room only. The music is good, mainly free and almost non-stop, with more than 200 separate acts. And the bedraggled hordes, specially if it is wet, find the whole thing irresistible. The Festival of Kerry is a long way from the ball gown and black tie event which circles in a different orbit.'

The Robinson report noted the confusion over the festival's name – The Rose of Tralee Festival or The Festival of Kerry. It found that it was relying heavily on publicity generated by its glamour events, rather than engaging in proper marketing. The festival was stuck in a rut.

'Media representatives get bored with ordinary routine and "nice" stories and inevitably seek controversy and scandal,' Robinson concluded. He advocated that a proper marketing programme should be set up, and suggested that the festival should adopt a more professional approach by replacing its volunteer structure with more paid employees.

Entertainers appearing in Tralee in 1995 included Mary Coughlin, Eleanor McEvoy, Niamh Kavanagh, Boyzone, Brendan Boyer, and An Emotional Fish. During the week that the festival was due to begin, Gay Byrne withdrew due to a health scare. The decision was taken so late that the RTÉ Guide was already published with him on the cover as the programme's compere.

He had always suggested that Mike Murphy would be his logical replacement. Mike had appeared a number of times on other programmes at the festival. Liam Miller, RTÉ's Director of Television, asked him to stand in. But Murphy would not do it.

'… it would be an act of hypocrisy on my part to present the show,' Murphy later wrote bluntly in his memoirs, *Mike and Me*.

'I really don't like the Rose of Tralee contest … purveying this particular Irish feminine ideal is a line that I for one, don't buy.'

Derek Davis was invited to do the programme, and he accepted the challenge. Born in Hollywood, County Down, he rose to national prominence by getting the only interview with US President Ronald Reagan during his 1984 visit to his ancestral village of Ballyporeen, County Tipperary. In 1994 Derek was compere at the Dubai Rose Selection, and he had also taken charge of the Ballybunion Bachelor Festival and the Mary of Dunloe contest.

Stepping in at the eleventh hour, he did particularly well in handling almost six hours of live television during the two nights.

The novel addition to the Roses was a contestant from South Africa, Victoria McLaren. She was born in Eastern Transvaal. Her father, Frank, was a mining engineer from Sligo.

The winner was Nyomi Horgan, 22, from Perth, a student of public relations and a part time model. She sang 'Waltzing Matilda' on stage and ended up as the bookies favourite at 4 to 1. Her escort actually placed a £180 bet on her at 8 to 1.

For the first time since the inception of the festival, parking was not a problem in Tralee. The number of people on the streets was significantly down, but the tuxedo and evening dress elements were

Below: Nyomi Horgan is serenaded as Rose of Tralee Across, from top: Colleen Mooney holds the Canadian flag as she is crowned Rose of Tralee 1996; Derek Davis took over as compere in 1995

❧ The winner was Nyomi Horgan

attracting more attention than ever. Guests at the Rose Ball included the Australian, Canadian, New Zealand and Nigerian ambassadors.

An average of thirty-two people came with each Rose, and they accounted for 6,500 bed nights during the week. As a result many of those coming for the race meeting had to find accommodation elsewhere, usually in Killarney, or Ballybunion.

❦ 1996 ❦

In early 1996 Gay Byrne announced that he would not compere the Rose of Tralee again, but he did agree to be a judge for that year's contest. Derek Davis was again selected to host the programme.

Radio Kerry reported on April 1, 1996 that Mary O'Connor, the original 19th century Rose of Tralee had been secretly married. Rather than laughing the whole thing off as the April Fool's joke that it was, the festival allowed it to be turned into a controversy over whether unmarried mothers would be ineligible to compete for Rose of Tralee. Liam Twomey, the general secretary of the festival committee, went on RTÉ's 'Morning Ireland' to say that the committee had drawn a line in banning unmarried mothers. Was the festival planning virginity tests? he was asked. If single mothers were accepted, married mothers could then justifiably claim they were being discriminated against as well, he replied.

Columnist Miriam Lord covered both the Dingle Regatta and the Rose of Tralee that year. She got somewhat carried away on a flight of fantasy, however, in her report of the opening of Dingle regatta on the Sunday. Charlie Haughey was uncharacteristically late, she wrote. He had 'fallen off' his boat, the *Celtic Mist*, and had to be rescued by an air corps helicopter which supposedly winched down a man to haul up 'a pathetic looking, wet bundle of human being, to safety'.

'That's what happens when you are enjoying your retirement and have no responsibilities,' Miriam continued, 'You fall into the sea.'

On this occasion, it was Miriam Lord who went overboard and had to be rescued by The Boss. She had not meant people to take her joke seriously.

'I'm sick as a pig,' she wrote in an open letter of apology to Charles Haughey from Tralee next day. 'For the record, our former Taoiseach never fell off the *Celtic Mist*. He did not have to be rescued by the Air Corps.' If he had, it would have been front page news, with all kinds of reminders: the famous time that he fell off the horse, or crashed the car in Wicklow, or had to be rescued by the Baltimore lifeboat after his boat ran into the Mizen Head and sunk.

Dick Spring opened the festival for the third year in a row. On the way to Tralee, the Roses visited Cork for a civic reception. It was announced that the winning Rose would feature on the QVC television channel promoting Irish goods. An Bord Trachtala was hoping to sell up to $7 million worth of Irish goods on the programme, which had the potential of reaching 38 million customers in the United States.

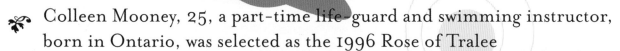

Colleen Mooney, 25, a part-time life-guard and swimming instructor, born in Ontario, was selected as the 1996 Rose of Tralee

Colleen Mooney, 25, a part-time life-guard and swimming instructor, born in Ontario, was selected as the 1996 Rose of Tralee. Both of her parents were from Dublin.

The TV ratings showed that the Tuesday and Wednesday night programmes had the highest viewing audience of any Irish programme that year, with over 950,000 viewers each night. There were some 60,000 extra adult viewers on the second night. This was offset by a drop in the number of younger viewers, as Network 2 was showing the concluding episode of 'The Fugitive', which set all kinds of records when first shown over thirty years earlier in 1967.

1997

Marty Whelan replaced Derek Davis as compere of the Rose Selection in 1997. The Roses gathered in advance in Dublin and attended the races at the Curragh in Kildare before going on to Waterford, where they visited the Waterford Crystal factory and stayed at Lismore Castle before arriving in Tralee for the Rose Ball.

The new Taoiseach, Bertie Ahern, officially opened the festival. Some sensed that he got particular pleasure out of upstaging his old adversary Dick Spring in the latter's own backyard. The festival was in competition with the Dingle Regatta and the Fleadh Cheoil in Listowel, which was attracting record crowds. In addition, Kerry were playing Meath in the all-Ireland senior football semi-final at Croke

Park. Kerry Group again provided a large screen as part of its annual Town Park Extravaganza.

The second night of Rose Selection had to be postponed for the first time ever, because of a hurricane-force storm. During the afternoon rehearsals the noise of the wind was so loud that 'some of the Roses couldn't hear themselves singing,' Marty Whelan explained.

People were particularly mindful of what happened to the Dome in 1983 when it came down in Hurricane Charlie. Although the new Dome was sturdier, that night's show was postponed. RTÉ put on a Batman film instead, and the second half of the selection was televised from the new Conference Centre at the Mount Brandon Hotel the following night.

Gay Byrne was one of the judges for a second year. Another judge was Noreen Cassidy, the Rose of 1986, who was Sales Manager with British Telecom.

Sydney Rose Yvette Jennifer McCloghry, 25, had been a police woman for four years. Her family originally came from Sligo in 1913, and she told of the horror of being jabbed with a needle by an HIV addict. The Cork Rose was Sinead Curtin, a niece of local Councillor John Wall, chairman of Tralee UDC. The winner was French Rose, Sinead Lonergan, who was a 16 to 1 outsider with the bookies. She was actually from Emly, County Tipperary, but had been working in Rennes, France, for the previous three years.

'One entrant snapped at another, who responded with what could only be called a vicious growl,' Grainne Cunningham reported. 'The judges frowned at this highly inappropriate behaviour for those

Across: 'Hands across the Sea' - the Washington Rose reaches out to Charles Haughey on board his yacht *The Celtic Mist*
Above, from top: Taoiseach Bertie Ahern, Gay Byrne and Marty Whelan sing Amhrán na bhFiann; Sinead Lonergan, Rose of Tralee 1997 is applauded

The winner was French Rose, Sinead Lonergan

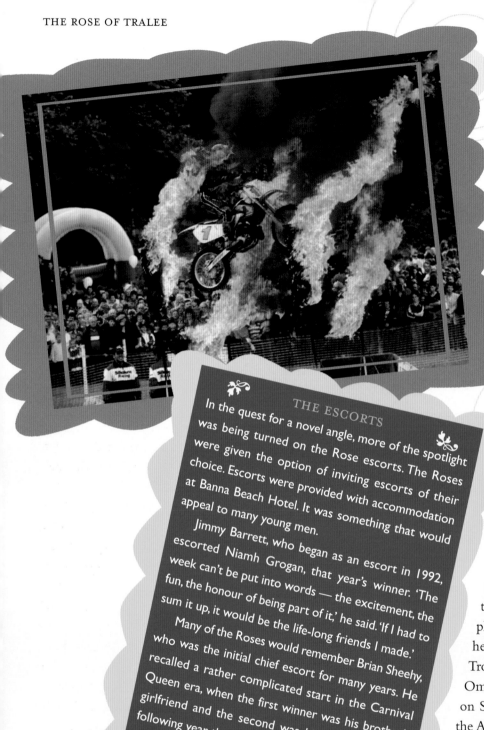

taking part in one of the country's most prestigious competitions. Their escorts were doing their best to prevent the atmosphere between the two entrants deteriorating any further.' The two were behaving like a couple of excitable bitches, which was fair comment, because Grainne was reporting on the international dog show that was run in conjunction with the festival!

❦ 1998 ❦

Festival President Seamus O'Halloran was a native of Belfast, so he hatched the idea of having the Roses assemble in Belfast, instead of Dublin, and then make their way down through the virtual length and breadth of the island in 1998. All the arrangements were made but on the week before this was to take place, the island was rocked by the heaviest loss of life of the whole Troubles with the bombing in Omagh by the so-called Real IRA on Saturday 15 August, the Feast of the Assumption, a Catholic holiday.

The Belfast trip was cancelled and the Roses went on an Italian tall ship *Orsa Maggiore*, which was in Dublin for the tall ships festival. Next they went to Robertstown by barge after visiting the Botanic Gardens in Glasnevin.

There was trouble among the festival organisers. Irreconcilable differences had developed between the festival's General

THE ESCORTS

In the quest for a novel angle, more of the spotlight was being turned on the Rose escorts. The Roses were given the option of inviting escorts of their choice. Escorts were provided with accommodation at Banna Beach Hotel. It was something that would appeal to many young men.

Jimmy Barrett, who began as an escort in 1992, escorted Niamh Grogan, that year's winner. 'The week can't be put into words — the excitement, the fun, the honour of being part of it,' he said. 'If I had to sum it up, it would be the life-long friends I made.'

Many of the Roses would remember Brian Sheehy, who was the initial chief escort for many years. He recalled a rather complicated start in the Carnival Queen era, when the first winner was his brother's girlfriend and the second was his own sister. The following year, the Tralee Rose was his second sister. And there was also the chance of romance. In 1967 Sean Dwyer was an escort when he first met Geraldine Healy, the Limerick Rose. They were on their honeymoon for the following year's Festival. The 1973 Rose, Veronica McCambridge married her local escort, Rowland Blennerhassett.

Secretary, Liam Twomey, and the board. This went into the High Court before the two sides settled. He was replaced, but then there would be a further dispute as to whether he was replaced on a professional or a voluntary basis. This new dispute gradually developed and played out in the background until the festival structure virtually imploded.

For a time the organisation seemed essentially rudderless. Noreen Cassidy, the Rose of 1986 and a former selection judge, was hired as the new General Secretary. She admitted that the festival was in need of a facelift.

Crowds were well down. 'It's easy to move around the street,' wrote Donal Hickey of the *Irish Examiner*. 'But fabulous entertainment can still be had, free of charge.' The free entertainment included Shane McGowan on stage in Denny Street, Liam Ó Maonlai of Hot House Flowers in the Town Park, while Van Morrison had a concert in the Brandon Conference Centre.

Luzveminda (Mindy) O'Sullivan, 21, a biochemistry student at Trinity College, Dublin, was chosen as Rose of Tralee. A great-grandfather on her father's side was a member of Kerry's first two all-Ireland winning football teams of 1903 and 1904, and a granduncle, Billy Myers, played on four all-Ireland winning Kerry teams from 1937 to 1941. Mindy's mother, Florita, was a Filipino who came to Ireland as an au pair for a Dublin family. She married Sean O'Sullivan, and they had five children, of whom Mindy was the eldest. Florita died when Mindy was ten years old. The entire family was in Tralee

Across: A spectacular motorbike stunt, 1998
Above, from top: Winning escort Donal Droney 2008 is shouldered high; a tearful Luzveminda O'Sullivan, Rose of Tralee 1998

Luzveminda O'Sullivan, 21, a biochemistry student at Trinity College, Dublin, was chosen as Rose of Tralee

Above: The new Rose, Luzveminda O'Sullivan with Lisa Brown

for the Rose of Tralee, and Mindy ended up a raging hot 2 to 1 favourite with the bookies.

The two nights of the television programme had the most popular and second most popular ratings for the year. Gay Byrne, who was one of the judges, noted that Mindy was the most popular winner he could remember. He had Mindy and her family on his 'Late Late Show' some days later when it came back on air after the summer recess. She told of how her father, who worked for Bord na Mona, had brought the family out to the Philippines to see their grandmother and other members of Florita's family after her death. Gay announced on the programme that the tissue company, Posies, was sponsoring a return visit to the Philippines for the whole family.

❦ 1999 ❦

Luzveminda O'Sullivan officially opened the 1999 festival as the reigning Rose of Tralee. It marked the 40th anniversary of the festival. A major feature on the opening night was a free open-air concert in front of the Ashe Memorial Hall, starring James Brown, renowned as 'The Godfather of Soul'. An estimated crowd of 13,000 turned up for the concert.

President Mary McAleese hosted a birthday party at the Earl of Desmond Hotel. 'The success of the festival is the success of many generations who have left our shores,' the President said. 'The challenges they faced were considerable but their links with their homeland were constant and were maintained by their love of Irish culture in all its forms.' The idea, which the founders of the festival fostered, had become a focal point for Irish communities throughout the world in places as far apart as Birmingham, Sydney and New York. Twenty former winners of the Rose of Tralee attended the dinner.

Luzveminda O'Sullivan became the first Rose of Tralee to associate herself formally with a charity for the year. She adopted Trocaire, which was active in the Philippines. Former Miss Ireland Olivia Tracy put on a fashion show during the 1999 festival; it raised £9,000 for Trocaire. Among the models were Luzveminda and Stanley Reilly, 25, from Clonmel, who was selected as Escort of the Year. He was an account manager with MinChem Environmental Services.

Below: Derek Davis enjoys a joke with Tara Lestor of Toronto in 1995
Bottom: Geraldine O'Grady, Rose of Tralee 1990

The Escort of the Year contest was introduced as a means of both fundraising and defraying expenses. Companies were asked to contribute £1,500 to sponsor an escort.

The longevity of the Rose of Tralee contest became particularly apparent in 1999 with the selection of Bridget Hope, 21, as the New Zealand Rose. Her mother had represented New Zealand in the contest as Paula Ryan exactly thirty years earlier. Japan entered its first Rose in 1999. The Rose, Amanda Ryan from Offaly, was indicative of the number of Irish people working in Japan. The Cork Rose, Geraldine O'Grady, 21, of Macroom was selected as Rose of Tralee. For her talent spot she gave a stirring rendition of the 'Tennessee Waltz'.

Cork Rose, Geraldine O'Grady, 21, of Macroom was selected as Rose of Tralee

After the Rose Selection Phil Coulter gave a piano recital, which included a duet with Clare Gallagher, 16, who was blinded by the Omagh bomb a year earlier. They got a standing ovation from the packed attendance. In addition, Christy Hennessy, who was a native of Tralee, held a homecoming concert.

In an effort to rectify the festival committee's financial position, the English committees were asked to contribute towards the upkeep

91

Above: Compere Marty Whelan
interviews the winner,
Geraldine O'Grady

of their Roses during the week in Tralee. The issue had been simmering since 1996 when the five British centres — London, Manchester, Leeds, Midlands, and south Wales — were asked to contribute £300 each towards their Rose's expenses, but they balked. These and other problems were then put on the long finger as the Festival committee ran up a debt of some £350,000. Although sizeable, this debt was less than half of the £850,000 annual budget. Each of the English Roses cost the Festival £3,100 in 1999, so the English centres were asked to pay IR£1,500 towards the following year's festival.

The various Rose centres were self-financing. Most had little difficulty raising money to cover the expenses of their own Rose selection contests. In Leeds, for example, the selection dinner dance essentially sold itself without any advertising. Attendance was limited to 500 people at £25 each, which raised £12,500, and the hotel charged £7,875. The organising committee would normally make a further £1,500 on a raffle. Other money was raised by selling advertising in a programme for the dinner. In addition, each of the English committees claimed to have generous commercial sponsorship, according to the *Irish Post*.

When the centres still would not contribute, the festival decided to reorganise its whole English operation by consolidating and upgrading the process with the selection of a single United Kingdom Rose in 2000.

At that point Norah Casey, the editor-in-chief of the *Irish Post*, invited each of the centres to send a girl to London, where the *Irish Post* was hosting a rival Rose Ball.

'I am fronting this publicity drive,' she told Myles Dungan on RTE. 'We will run, we will host, we will fund a Rose Ball.' She added that it was 'virtually impossible for the Festival to do anything without the support of the *Irish Post*.' The Irish Post held its ball and selected a winner, but she was a Rose to nowhere, and the breakaway fizzled out.

❧ THE NEW MILLENNIUM ❧

Noreen Cassidy injected a new enthusiasm and sought to control the spending and improve marketing. In 2000 there was a 25% increase in sponsorship and a major effort was made to increase the family appeal, with children's entertainment during the afternoon. Westlife had a free open air concert on Sunday night at the Ashe Memorial Hall, and they also appeared in the Dome for Rose Selection, which apparently improved the appeal of the programme, because it attracted a record rating of 1.3 million TV viewers who watched Roisin Egenton of New York being chosen as Rose of Tralee.

❧ Roisin Egenton of New York being chosen as Rose of Tralee

The festival received £10,000 from Bord Fáilte for its award-winning website in 2000 and £25,000 from the Millennium Committee, which had given the festival £50,000 the previous year.

❧ 2001 ❧

The Rose of Tralee for 2001 was Lisa Manning) of Perth, Australia. Her father, Michael, was a plumbing contractor from Kilbride, County Meath. Lisa recited a poem written by her English mother that was loosely based on the lines from Shakespeare's *Romeo and Juliet*. 'What's in a name? That which we call a rose, By any other name would smell as sweet.'

The human-interest story that captured the public imagination that year was told to Marty Whelan by one of Lisa's Australian counterparts, Aimee Butler of Adelaide, the South Australian Rose. Born in Taiwan, she was adopted by a couple from Adelaide, Ian and Susan Butler, who both traced their roots to Ireland. Aimee grew up without knowing about her birth parents until three years earlier when she traced her birth mother and visited her in Taiwan.

Above, from top: Roisin Ryan Egenton, Rose of Tralee 2000 is applauded by the other Roses; Marty Whelan looks for some beauty tips!

❧ The Rose of Tralee for 2001 was Lisa Manning of Perth, Australia

Above: Lisa Manning, Rose of Tralee 2001
Across, from top: Tamara Gervasoni, Rose of Tralee 2002; Kerry football supporters in full regalia

'When I met her I could see the sadness in her eyes, I could see the regret,' she explained. 'But, you know, I wanted to comfort her to let her know that things had been good for me. I was almost glad that she gave me up because I had been blessed so much with my parents in Australia and I love them so much.'

In 2001 the Government allocated €31.75 million as part of a Festival-Cultural events initiative for the entire country. Killarney, which was in the constituency of Arts Minister John O'Donoghue, was allocated over €480,000 for a new Summerfest, and in the budget of December 2001 the then Minister for Finance announced the allocation of €320,000 for the Rose of Tralee Festival as a once-off gesture 'in recognition of the role of the festival in generating tourism in the region'.

The allocation was undoubtedly a tribute to the marketing skills of Noreen Cassidy, but it sparked a degree of controversy. When the media sought details under the Freedom of Information Act, an official at the Department of Finance would only say that it was unusual for there to be such a paucity of records in relation to a spending decision. But the Celtic Tiger economy was roaring at the time and government money was being doled out at an exceptional rate to various events.

❦ 2002 ❦

The festival was faced with an unprecedented rival attraction in 2002 when Kerry were scheduled to meet Cork for the first time ever in an all-Ireland football semi-final. The timing presented a major challenge. The festival sought to pull out the stops by engaging

Phil Coulter to play a free open-air concert on Denny Street but it had to be postponed until the following night as the safety authorities felt the stage was not sturdy enough for the likely crowd.

There were entrants from three new centres in 2002: Italy, Luxembourg, and Philadelphia. Tamara Gervasoni, whose mother hailed from Longford, represented Italy. Yvonne Linterr, the Luxemburg Rose, was born in Dublin, while the Dubai Rose, Zena al Nazer, was also born in Dublin. Her mother was from Bantry, County Cork, but there was no doubting her Arab blood.

Tamara Gervasoni of Italy was selected Rose of Tralee but shortly afterwards she was arrested for shoplifting. It transpired that she was suffering from bulimia. But as a result of Noreen Cassidy's astute handling of this very sensitive and personal issue, the festival committee was presented with an award at the Consultants Association Awards Ceremony the following year.

❧ Tamara Gervasoni of Italy was selected Rose of Tralee

Income from the Dome was €188,734, but Dome expenditure was €238,113, with the result that it lost almost €50,000 in an area where it should have been making most money. There was no income from the street entertainment, which cost over €275,000

With the festival organisation plagued by infighting and debt, Noreen Cassidy decided to move on. She had already given her notice, but in her final week a document was circulated to the local media that was in some respects grossly defamatory. Most of the items cited were verifiable facts, but these were interspersed with some distortions about Noreen Cassidy that could easily be discredited. It was a classic case of the old adage — the greater the truth, the greater the libel.

95

Below: Compere Ryan Tubridy with Kerry Rose Olivia Dineen
Bottom: Orla Tobin, Rose of Tralee 2003
Across, from top: 'I've got my eye on that crown!' Orla O'Shea with young admirers; Orla was chosen as Rose of Tralee 2004

The *Kerryman* received the document shortly before going to press. The editor happened to be away, but a report based on the document made its way onto the front page of the last edition. The allegations were withdrawn with a full apology the following week. However, the person lined up to succeed Noreen as General Secretary turned down the job as a result.

❦ 2003 ❦

The festival limped on for another year. After six years hosting the Rose of Tralee, Marty Whelan was replaced by Ryan Tubridy of RTE.

In his first year Ryan Tubridy not only hosted the Rose Selection but also officially opened the festival. The opening was followed by a free open-air concert featuring the Hot House Flowers on the platform of the Ashe Memorial Hall.

The dress affairs were becoming pricier than ever. The Rose Ball was now €100 a ticket and the festival no longer paid for Fossett's circus. Instead of the 10p charged for entry over many years, the charge was increased to €10 each, and tickets for the Rose Selection were €30 each. Nevertheless, the festival was in more serious debt than ever.

Dublin Rose Orla Tobin was chosen as Rose of Tralee. She was the last winner under the old voluntary committee system, which had prevailed since 1959. It had become very obvious that if it were to survive, the festival would have to be run in future on a sound commercial basis.

❧ Dublin Rose Orla Tobin was chosen as Rose of Tralee.

Siobhan Hanley, who took over as General Secretary from Noreen Cassidy in late 2002, approached Anthony O'Gara for help. 'She was trying to get people involved,' he explained. 'As my main talent is in restructuring business, I said I would give it a go. They asked me to look at the structure of it and see if I could develop a five year plan, and I became involved on that basis.' O'Gara had worked in the Kerry Group for fourteen years before setting up his own consultancy operation in Tralee in 1996.

'I turned to a few people I knew and asked for their support. They agreed as long as I would manage the company myself for the next few years.'

❦ 2004 ❦

As of September 30, 2003 the festival committee accepted that it owed €900,153 and it sought to restructure in order to avoid bankruptcy by paying all creditors 30%. The overwhelming majority agreed to this arrangement and the whole operation was reorganized and the company was formally registered on April 14, 2004 as Kerry Rose Festival Limited, trading as Rose of Tralee International Festival.

The main shareholders in the new company were Anthony O'Gara, Ciaran Desmond, a commercial lawyer in Cork city, John McCarthy, an accountant living in Tralee, Maurice Quaid from Limerick, who was running a food distributing business in the Southeast, and Michael Quaid from Limerick who was living in Cork.

'We looked at how we might run things more effectively and efficiently and that involved using less expenditure and bringing in more income,' O'Gara explained. They set up a five-year plan to introduce more Rose centres. They aimed to increase the number of overseas centres to a total of 85. Obviously it would not be possible to have eighty-five Roses competing in the final, so he planned a series of regional selections in Ireland. His plan was to expand on the festival's initial setup in selecting the Kerry Rose with heats throughout Kerry, except that this time there would be contestants from each of the thirty-two counties of Ireland. Ultimately the plan was to whittle those down to six or seven regional Irish Roses.

The overall number of Roses was cut back to 26 in 2004, with 11 of those coming from Ireland. Laois, Kildare and Kilkenny sent contestants for the first time. The winner was Orla O'Shea, 20, from Kilkenny. Ryan Tubridy was again compere.

❦ The winner was Orla O'Shea, 20, from Kilkenny

❦ 2005 ❦

The Roses finally made it to Northern Ireland in 2005. Their tour began in Armagh, from where they went on to Derry and then to Belfast, before flying to Cork and going on to Tralee by bus.

As a private business the festival did not enjoy the extensive sponsorship of previous years so it was decided to concentrate on five or six key sponsors, and to make dramatic savings in a number of areas.

The Dome was moved from its traditional location in the main Brandon Hotel car park, as it cost at least €25,000 annually. In 2004 it was erected in the parking lot at the back of the Brandon Hotel, which was a confined space that cut down dramatically on security costs.

Oliver Hurley managed the entertainment programme and cut the previous budget in half. The new festival organizers recognized that it was no longer economically possible to put on the same kind of show on the streets as the festival was competing with other attractions around the country. They did not go for major names on the streets, but Christy Hennessy and Frances Black held a concert in the Dome.

Crowds in the streets over the week were a pale shadow of former years, but the televised aspects were stronger than ever.

Compere of Rose Selection had become one of the most coveted spots on television, because it enjoyed such high ratings. The profile of the host of the show was considerably enhanced, and he would find himself in great demand for other programmes in the following weeks. Ray D'Arcy took on the mantle of compere in 2005 and his ease with

🌿 The smart money was on the Mayo Rose, Aoibhinn Ní Shúilleabháin (22) to win the title, and she duly became the Rose of Tralee.

Across, from top: Rose of Tralee 2005, Aoibhinn Ní Shúilleabháin with Kerry County Library staff; Aoibhinn studies form at the races
Below: Kathryn Feeney, Rose of Tralee 2006 is congratulated
Bottom: Cork and Kerry roses don each other's colours

the participants proved a great success.

From the outset the smart money was on the Mayo Rose, Aoibhinn Ní Shúilleabháin (22) to win the title, and she duly became the Rose of Tralee. She had a degree with first class honours in theoretical physics from University College Dublin.

'Over two evenings the Roses proved a show that had been written-off as dated, patronising and irrelevant, contained more wit, life and talent than an entire season of "You're a Star",' Kathy Sheridan noted in *The Irish Times*. Her judgment was supported by the viewing numbers, which were up by more than a quarter over the previous year. Some 881,000 people watched the programme, the highest audience since 2000. The audience was second only to the live final of 'You're A Star'.

🌿 2006 🌿

The selection of the 2006 Rose of Tralee went out live on the Internet. Again there was keen competition over the weekend, because Cork and Kerry were meeting in the all-Ireland football semi-final at Croke Park.

There was heavy betting on the South Australian Rose, Niamh O'Reilly, who became second favourite when her odds tumbled from 66 to 1 to just 4 to 1 after she performed a very funny skit on stage, adopting the voice of a cartoon character called Joo Joo Eyeballs. New Zealand Rose Emma Coffey performed a Maori tribal dance, which involved swinging luminous balls around her head, but the bookies' favourite, Queensland Rose Kathryn Feeney, was chosen as the 48th Rose of Tralee.

🌿 Queensland Rose Kathryn Feeney, was chosen as the 48th Rose of Tralee

❦ 2007 ❦

Below: Lisa Murtagh, Rose of
Tralee 2007

The following year on the weekend of the festival the Rolling
Stones were playing in concert at Slane. It was getting more difficult
to compete and also to attract media attention.

Publican Bill Kirby, who was celebrating his 30th festival since
taking over the famous Brogue Inn in Tralee, had been
a constant supporter of the festival, putting up
thousands where others subscribed little more than a
pittance. He did his best to drum up coverage.

'Give us some good publicity,' he asked some
visiting reporters. 'This is unique, there's nothing like
it anywhere in the world,' he said. Unfortunately it
was to be Bill's last festival.

Texas Rose, Megan Foley, was accompanied by
a somewhat unusual group. Her parents were
divorced and had remarried other people, so
Megan's supporters included her mother and
stepfather, and her father and stepmother. Her
father, Chuck Foley, told how his great-great-
grandfather had gone to the United States from
Cork in 1858. Although no Texas Rose ever
won, the men in the Texas contingent were
always highly distinguishable in black Stetson
hats and cowboy boots. All they were lacking
were the horses and six-shooters.

Lisa Murtagh, 27, of New York was selected
at the 49th Rose of Tralee in 2007. She was a
practicing attorney and was the favourite with
the bookies from the outset. The programme
was again considered a great success for Ray
D'Arcy who adopted a mocking blend of wit
and warmth. Although the viewing audience
had dipped to 573,000 in 2006, it was up by
over 26% to 724,000 in 2007.

Shortly after the festival the shareholders
of Ballybeggan Park decided to sell the racecourse for housing
development. This was expected to spell the end of horse racing in
Tralee, which could trace races back to 1767. Ballybeggan Park was

❦ Lisa Murtagh, 27, of New York was selected at the 49th
Rose of Tralee in 2007

Above: The 2007 Rose with earlier Roses of Tralee (from left, back) Brenda Hyland 1983, Sinead Boyle 1989, Ann Foley 1967, Therese Gillespie 1965, Coleen Mooney 1996, Josie Ruane 1961, Denise Murphy 1991; (front) Sinead Lonergan 1997, Lisa Murtagh 2007, Orla O'Shea 2004

opened as a racecourse in 1898. In 1982 the famous Dawn Run – the most successful race mare in the history of National Hunt racing – won her first race in Tralee, with her owner, Charmian Hill, in the saddle. Another famous winner in Tralee was Vintage Crop, which won the Carling Gold Cup in 1992 and went on to become the first foreign-trained horse to win the Melbourne Cup in Australia. Desert King also won his first race in Tralee in 1996 before going on to win the Irish Derby the following year. In addition, Aidan O'Brien had his first winner in Tralee as trainer in 1993.

With the expected demise of the racecourse the business community in Tralee had to take stock of the festival. Times had changed, but the festival had not changed with the times. Many of the businesses began to realise that they were losing out as the crowds declined. They would undoubtedly be hit further with the loss of the race meetings. The bands formula had gone and while big international names created an extra draw, the cost had become prohibitive, as was the cost of public liability insurance. Some of those spending the money had little appreciation of the difficulty in collecting it.

Gay Byrne had warned committee members years earlier that they were getting the reputation of being the softest touch in the entertainment business. They not only hired expensive personalities but also paid to put up their friends. The festival committee also put up the Rose escorts, but this had begun to be put on a commercial footing, with escorts having to raise €2,000 in sponsorship money. In 2007 there were some 250 inquiries about being escorts and 95 young men applied. Fifty-five were interviewed and they were whittled down to 31 escorts and 6 reserves. The money more than covered their upkeep for the week, as they were housed in student accommodation available for tourist purposes during college holidays.

❧ 2008 ❧

A major change in the Rose eligibility rules took place in the run-up to the 2008 Festival. For the first time unmarried mothers were allowed to participate. Anthony O'Gara said it was important to move with the times. 'I know some people who say they're role models, but we don't think a woman is any less of a person because she happens to have a child,' he said. 'We are proud to reflect that's part of the world we live in, and we want to live in the real world.'

Just as different entities such as horse racing, dog racing, the dog show, and golf competitions had run separately over the years with only the loosest connection to the festival committee, the new festival structure divided into two separate entities in 2008. The local vintners took over the old street carnival aspect. Since the 1960s the festival committee had complained that some of the businesses in town were not pulling their weight. They were the main beneficiaries of the street scene and some contributed very little, so the street entertainment was largely handed over to the vintners, but they were subsidised by the Rose of Tralee company, which paid for the street lighting, parades and fireworks.

Tipperary Rose Aoife Kelly, 23, from Portroe, was selected as the Rose of Tralee in

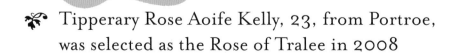

❧ Tipperary Rose Aoife Kelly, 23, from Portroe, was selected as the Rose of Tralee in 2008

2008. An occupational therapist, she worked in the spinal injury service in the National Rehabilitation Institute. With her bubbly personality she was 7 to 4 favourite to win the title.

❦ 2009 ❦

The 50th anniversary of the foundation of the Rose of Tralee will see fifty Roses from ten countries: 5 from Australia, 13 from Britain, 4 from Canada, 9 from Ireland, 14 from the United States, and a Rose each from Dubai, France, Germany, Luxembourg and New Zealand. In addition, the winners from 1959 onwards have been invited back and over forty are expected. There will be an exhibition of the dresses worn by the winning Roses, a special TV documentary, and a mega concert featuring Sharon Shannon, The Saw Doctors, Shane McGowan, Damien Dempsey. Tralee will be *en fete* for the entire period, but the highlight, as it has been for half a century, will be the selection of the Rose of Tralee, when, once again, the famous opening lines will be heard:

'The pale moon was rising above the green mountain...'

Across: Aoife Kelly, Rose of Tralee 2008
Above: Compere Ray D'Arcy gets to grips with Cork Rose Niamh O'Hanlon
Right: Alice O'Sullivan, the very first Rose of Tralee in 1959, joined forces with the 2008 Rose to announce plans for the 50th anniversary celebrations in 2009

Epilogue

The Festival of Kerry undoubtedly did more for the image of Tralee during the third quarter of the twentieth century than any other event. Unlike Killarney, which was a tourist attraction going back to the Victorian era, Tralee was not even a tourist way-station in the early 1950s. Over the ensuing decades the Rose of Tralee Festival essentially provided Tralee with a brand that put the town on the tourist map and vitalised a neglected part of Ireland. The driving forces within the festival did not become active in local or national politics, though people like Florence O'Connor and Denis Reen were approached. Denis became involved in the construction of Tralee Golf Course at Barrow and the Aqua Dome, and he was also brought in to rescue the Jeanie Johnston famine ship project. Margaret Dwyer went to demonstrate her competence in the promotion of tourism as Sales Manager of the Mount Brandon Hotel, and Dick O'Sullivan exhibited his organisational talents as head of Bord na gCon and Manager of Punchestown Race Course.

Above: Stalwarts of the Old Brigade

They and others had contributed to transforming Tralee in the first half-century of the Rose of Tralee Festival. The original organisers and those volunteers who worked tirelessly behind the scenes were undoubtedly a huge factor in the success of the festival and its longevity. Although the festival is now on a more businesslike footing, it has retained its image as an occasion for joy, fun and innocent entertainment – a remarkable achievement, especially during the years of Celtic Tiger sophistication and hype.

Researching the origins and events of the festival has revived many happy memories and resurrected images of people and places that deserve a place in the story of Tralee.

I hope that for all of those who participated in the festival, as Roses, escorts, supporters, entertainers, or who simply enjoyed the fabulous fun it provided, this book will be a treasured memento of wonderful times – and an encouragement to take part in the wonderful times ahead.

A final word from Anthony O'Gara, Managing Director of The International Rose of Tralee Festival

They were obviously exceptional people. Kerry people have a reputation for being canny and pragmatic but these gentlemen took it to a higher level.

I have experience of the more familiar routine: meet the lads in the pub, have a few pints, gradually realise that with your combined imagination a great idea has taken shape. Obviously, by the time we are back to our full health, the idea doesn't seem so clever after all.

The gentlemen who met in Harty's Bar fifty years ago were made of different stuff. It's remarkable to realise as we celebrate fifty years of this wonderful festival just how much the town of Tralee owes to the foresight of those people.

The celebrations to mark the fifty years of the Rose of Tralee International Festival give us and the people of Tralee an opportunity to say 'thank you' and 'welcome home' to our returning friends who have enjoyed the Festival over the years and who wish to relive the many great memories.

We salute everyone who has played a part in organising the Festival since its foundation in 1959. These people, mostly volunteers, have been the cord connecting Tralee and Ireland with Irish communities all over world.

Roses of Tralee act as our Festival's ambassadors and the manner in which they do so is the cornerstone of our success. They are, of course, lovely and fair, but self-evidently it is not their beauty alone that wins hearts and minds annually. They continue to inspire us with their intelligence, confidence and sense of fun.

Rose Centres around the world have trebled in the past five years which underlines the continuing passion for the Rose of Tralee in Irish communities abroad and in our thirty-two counties at home.

Above: Anthony O'Gara with a selection of 2004 Roses including winner Orla O'Shea

The Rose of Tralee has been very good for tourism in Ireland. The Festival generates a huge amount of publicity and goodwill for Tralee and Kerry on an annual basis. This tradition started in 1959 when Movietone and Pathé brought the Festival to a wider audience, and it continues to attract immense media coverage, primarily as a leading programme on the RTÉ schedule, attracting one million viewers. It also enjoys immense coverage in the local, national and regional press. This coverage has allowed us to attract tremendous sponsorship to the Festival over the years, and our present lead sponsor, Newbridge Silverware, continue that great tradition. All sponsoring companies realise that they are tapping into a very successful brand – The Rose of Tralee.

In conclusion, I wish to thank everyone who has been involved in building and sustaining this great Festival over the past fifty years. We are privileged to continue this work and we have very exciting plans for the future development of the Festival. However, our focus remains constant: 'To celebrate and connect the Global Irish Community every year in Tralee.'

Anthony O'Gara

LIST OF ENTRANTS AND WINNERS

Each year's Rose of Tralee is highlighted in red.

1959

Birmingham	Maura Browne
DUBLIN	ALICE O'SULLIVAN
London	Angela Flynn
New York	Sheila Ann Horgan
Tralee	Kathleen Sheehy

1960

Birmingham	Kathleen Clifford
Boston	Kathleen Nash
CHICAGO	TERESA KENNY
Dublin	Joan Cronin
Kerry	Sheila Fitzgerald
Leeds	Teresa Teahan
London	Maureen Scully
New York	Joan Dineen
Tralee	Mary O'Shea

1961

Birmingham	Una Murphy
Boston	Alice O'Leary
Chicago	Nora Reidy
CORK	JOSIE RUANE
Dublin	Eileen McMahon
Kerry	Mary Egan
Leeds	Bridie Godley
Limerick	Maralene McCarthy
London	Anne Tangney
New York	Maureen Sheehan
Tralee	Margaret Kerins

1962

Birmingham	Philomena Gallagher
Boston	Ita Slattery
Chicago	Kathleen Brosnan
Cork	Maureen Carroll
DUBLIN	CIARA O'SULLIVAN
Kerry	Eileen Garvey
Leeds	Eileen O'Connor
Limerick	Kathleen O'Flaherty
London	Rena Coffey
New York	Myra Byrne
San Francisco	Elizabeth McCloy
Tralee	Morna Williams

1963

Birmingham	Bridie Murphy
BOSTON	GERALDINE FITZGERALD
Chicago	Eileen Lynch
Cork	Gwen Byrne
Coventry	Mary Boyle
Dublin	Elizabeth Hickson
Kerry	Maura Smith
Limerick	Betty O'Carroll
London	Carol Murphy
Manchester	Frances Larkin
New York	Patricia McGillycuddy
San Francisco	Fidelma O'Kelly
Sydney	Catherine McCarthy
Tralee	Pat Chute

1964

Belfast	Una Quigley
Birmingham	Doreen O'Connor
Boston	Marie King
Chicago	Mary Kavanagh
Cork	Eleanor Dineen
Dublin	Elizabeth Lucey
Kerry	Breda Gaine
Limerick	Helena Naughton
London	Margaret Fitzmaurice
Manchester	Barbara McKenna
New York	Mary Kelaher
San Francisco	Catherine Walsh
Sydney	Noreen Browne
TRALEE	MARGARET O'KEEFFE

1965

BELFAST	THERESE GILLESPIE
Birmingham	Ina O'Mahony
Boston	Maureen Sheehy
Chicago	Mary Brosnan
Cork	Eleanor O'Callaghan
Dublin	Irene Courtney
Kerry	Mary O'Sullivan
Leeds	Margaret Byrne
London	Patricia Gabbett
Manchester	Pauline Lowry
New York	Bridget O'Sullivan
San Francisco	Dawn Hartnett

Sydney	Isobelle Hyland
Toronto	Eileen Kearney
Tralee	Helen Purcell

1966

Belfast	Carol Parker
Birmingham	Mary O'Connor
Boston	Kathleen O'Donnell
Cork	Jacqueline Purcell
Detroit	Kathleen Sheehan
Dublin	Maura Enright
Kerry	Eleanor O'Connor
Leeds	Madeleine Gison
Limerick	Bernie McElligott
London	Bernadette Casey
Manchester	Sheila Fitzpatrick
New York	Elizabeth Farley
NEW ZEALAND	LORAINE STOLLERY
San Francisco	Margaret Larkin
Toronto	Collette O'Sullivan
Tralee	Mary Ruane

1967

Belfast	Eithne Downey
BIRMINGHAM	ANN FOLEY
Boston	Ruth Begley
Cork	Eilish McSweeney
Detroit	Carol Ann Reardon
Dublin	Rosaleen Kelliher
Galway	Mary Manning
Kerry	Jean Moloney
Leeds	Georgina Bird
Limerick	Geraldine Healy
Liverpool	Noreen Lyne
London	Marie Hobley
Manchester	Ann Murphy
New York	Hanna Marie Carmody
New Zealand	Sharon Cameron
San Francisco	Catherine O'Mahony
Toronto	Mary O'Donoghue
Tralee	Margaret O'Rahilly

1968

Belfast	Ann Lynagh
Birmingham	Ann Doherty
Boston	Mary Quigley
Chicago	Kathleen Casey
CLARE	EILEEN SLATTERY
Cork	Ann Galvin
Detroit	Kathy Ann Taylor
Dublin	Kay Kavanagh

France	Georgina Gerassi
Kerry	Doreen Brosnan
Leeds	Barbara Bentley
Limerick	Aileen Nugent
Liverpool	Olive Carragher
London	Sally Murphy
Los Angeles	Deirdre O'Reilly
New York	Kathleen McLaughlin
New Zealand	Margaret O'Loan
Nottingham	Moira O'Connell
Philadelphia	Ann O'Reilly
San Francisco	Judith Hardiman
Sydney	Carmel Shannon
Toronto	Kathleen O'Sullivan
Waterford	Marion Nagle

1969

Argentina	Martha E. McLoughlin
Belfast	Patricia Mary Harney
Birmingham	Una Marie Molloy
Boston	Mary J. Mullarkey
Clare	Melissa Mary Byrne
Cork	Clare Levis
Detroit	Mary Early
DUBLIN	CATHY QUINN
France	Martine Brohan
Holyoake	Debbie Kennedy
Kerry	Breda Finnegan
Leeds	Catherine Loft
Limerick	Mary Ryan
Liverpool	Deirdre P. Doran
London	Pauline Tyrell
Melbourne	Sandra E. Briggs
New York	Terry Mark Burke
New Zealand	Paula Ryan
Nottingham	Margaret Kelly
Toronto	Sheila Mary O'Reilly
Tralee	Ann O'Mahony
Waterford	Germaine Baily

1970

Belfast	Denise McCluskey
Birmingham	Angela Timlin
Boston	Marie Berard
Chicago	Katherine Hughes
Clare	Ann Maria Hanrahan
Cork	Marie Foley
Dublin	Evelyn Barden
HOLYOKE	KATHLEEN WELSH
Kerry	Niamh Murray
Leeds	Maureen Flaherty

London	Haley Waterworth
Melbourne	Joan Hannon
Miami	Peg Nugent
Michigan	Kathleen Sullivan
New York	Noreen Culhane
New Zealand	Anne McConnell
San Francisco	Kerry Wair
Sydney	Monica Heary
Toronto	Catherine O'Brien
Waterford	Vera Walsh

1971

Belfast	Patricia O'Connell
Birmingham	Noreen Moriarty
Boston	Kathleen McDonough
Calgary	Molly Hammill
Chicago	Kathleen Sheehan
Clare	Catherine Turner
Cork	Bridget Walsh
Dublin	Margaret Foley
Holyoke	Ann Marie O'Brien
Kerry	Sandra O'Donoghue
Lawrence	Kathleen Dynan
Leeds	Maureen Gibbons
Limerick	Aine Devane
Liverpool	Mary Walsh
London	Patricia Sugrue
Melbourne	Mary Dowling
MIAMI	LINDA MCCRAVY
Michigan	Linda McCarthy
New York	Tracy Halloran
New Zealand	Bronwyn Gill
San Francisco	Jane McCabe
Sydney	Anne Teahan
Thames Valley	Linda Heneghan
Toronto	Lilian Dowling
Tyneside	Moira Duffy
Waterford	Ronnie Cuffe

1972

Adelaide	Patricia Sullivan
Belfast	Anne Crockford
Birmingham	Margaret Tierney
Boston	Christina Marie Daly
Chicago	Eileen Hennigan
Clare	Catherine O'Sullivan
Cork	Mary Corbett
Dublin	Lucy Jones
France	Veronique Bernard
Hawaii	Kathleen Puanani O'Sullivan
Holland	Nuala Malone

Kerry	June Stack
Lawrence	Patricia Sullivan
Leeds	Kathleen McGee
Limerick	Carol Cashman
Liverpool	Deirdre Murphy
London	Annette Murphy
Melbourne	Cecily O'Callaghan
Michigan	Beth Dingman
Holyoke	Nancy Rainville
New York	Mary Angela O'Neill
Newcastle-Upon-Tyne	Teresa Keating
Offaly	Dympna Dolan
San Francisco	Ann Jeanette Kelly
SWITZERLAND	CLAIRE FRANCES DUBENDORFER
Sydney	Margaret Nethery
Thames Valley	Denise Hutt
Toronto	Carmel O'Neill
Waterford	Christina Helen Laracy

1973

Adelaide	Catherine Barry
BELFAST	VERONICA MCCAMBRIDGE
Birmingham	Sheelagh Smythe
Chicago	Teresa Gilmartin
Clare	Fionnuala Burna
Cork	Geraldine Rohan
Dublin	Jacqueline Hayes
Gaeltacht	Caitlin Ní Chonghaile
Holland	Alice Zurcher
Holyoke	Sherry McFadden
Kerry	Mary Adams
Leeds	Anne Greene
Limerick	Mary Kelly
London	Noreen Moriarty
Melbourne	Annette Mulvihill
Montreal	Cheryl Heffernan
New York	Marybeth Spanarkel
New Zealand	Nicolette Prendergast
Newcastle-Upon-Tyne	Patricia Gallagher
Offaly	Bernadette Claffey
San Francisco	Deirdre Kennedy
Switzerland	Marianne Gorey
Sydney	Karlene Beath
Thames Valley	Eva Marie Lynch
Toronto	Diane Mulholland
Tralee	Joy Hanbridge
Waterford	Catherine Hayes

1974

Adelaide	Marian Malloy

Belfast	Rosaleen McErlane
Birmingham	Pauline Griffin
Chicago	Roseann Finnegan
Cork	Kathleen Leslie
Dublin	Eithne Malone
Holland	Helen Snowdon
Holyoke	Mary Ann Croke
Kerry	Noreen O'Sullivan
Leeds	Mary Brown
Limerick	Mary Barry
London	Maria Barry
Melbourne	Susal Wynne
Michigan	Theresa McGrath
NEW YORK	MARGARET FLAHERTY
New Zealand	Francesca Deegan
Newcastle-Upon-Tyne	Caitriona Steward
Offaly	Rosemary Mannion
San Francisco	Colleen Sapper
Switzerland	Nora Escher
Sydney	Catherine Starr
Toronto	Philomena Connaghton
Tralee	Eileen Daly
Washington	Aimee Ewers
Waterford	Beryl Fitzgerald

1975

Adelaide	Angela Atkinson
Belfast	Dorothy Maguire
Birmingham	Bernadette McCool
Cailín Gaelach	Máire Nic Ghiolla Easpaig
Chicago	Maire Bryner
Cork	Elizabeth Connolly
Dublin	Marie Gilmartin
Galway	Mary Callanan
Holland	Joe-Anne Blance Raby
Holyoke	Martha Marie Donohue
Kerry	Margaret Savage
LONDON	MAUREEN SHANNON
Melbourne	Colleen O'Donnell
Michigan	Maureen Gordon
New York	Helen Theresa Healy
New Zealand	Glenise Margaret Carruthers
Newcastle-On-Tyne	Linda O'Kane
Ohio	Marian O'Donnell
Pennsylvania	Ann Curran
Peterborough	Mary Leahy
San Francisco	Marcia Ward
Toronto	Vicki Thurston
Tralee	Noelle Corridan
Washington D.C.	Kimberly Tobin
Waterford	Mevra Stapleton

1976

Adelaide	Bernadette Murphy
Belfast	Pauline Thompson
Birmingham	Mary Mullen
Cailín Gaelach	Máire Ní Cheallaigh
Chicago	Maureen Payne
Cork	Helen Kealy
Dublin	Ann Maken
Galway	Eithne Kennedy
Holyoke	Ann Able
Kerry	Caragh Evans
Leeds	Maureen Harte
Limerick	Ann Jones
London	Rose Marie Sorohan
Melbourne	Adele Hanafin
Michigan	Carrie Hall
NEW YORK	MARIE SODEN
New Zealand	Jane Walker
Ohio	Sissy McKenna
Pennsylvania	Jeanne Newell
Peterborough	Cathy Moher
San Francisco	Colleen Philpott
Sydney	Maura Quinn
Toronto	Caroline King
Tralee	Ann McCrohan
Washington D.C.	Joan Hanlon
Waterford	Deirdre Jones

1977

Belfast	Margaret Mary McKeague
Birmingham	Mary Theresa NcNulty
Cailín Gaelach	Mairead Ní Dhonnachu
Chicago	Catherine Mary O'Connell
Cork	Paula Marie Byrne
Dublin	Geraldine Flanaghan
Galway	Mary Geraldine Diskin
Holland	Rosabel Elizabeth Everard
Holyoke	Patricia Marie Dean
Jersey	Marie McCann
Kerry	Susan Geraldine Feighan
Las Vegas	Patricia Ellen Matyas
Leeds	Gail Margaret Curtis
Limerick	Adrienne McCrory
London	Elaine Ann Tully
Michigan	Jeanne Marie Selander
New York	Eileen Frances Burke
New Zealand	Susanne Norris
Ohio	Mary Talty
Peterborough	Mary Catherine Herlihy
San Francisco	Eileen Moore
Sydney	Julie Maria Bergin

Thames Valley	Angela Regina Norry
Toronto	Patricia Alice O'Shea
Tralee	Maureen Bridget Kennelly
Washington D.C.	Jean Marie Kearns Jorgensen
WATERFORD	ORLA BURKE

1978

Belfast	Geraldine McGrinder
Birmingham	Cassie Collins
Cailín Gaelach	Mairead Ní Pheoil
Chicago	Kerry Lynan
Cork	Fiona Ní Chleirigh
Dublin	Barbara Cluskey
Galway	Monica Collins
Holland	Maureen Balsters
Holyoke	Kate Quirk
Jersey	Angela Gribben
Kerry	Vera Foley
Las Vegas	Siobhan O'Carroll
Leeds	Bernadette Walsh
Limerick	Deirdre Moore
London	Rosaleen Garvey
Michigan	Cynthia O'Connor
New York	Maureen Doyle
New Zealand	Catherine Kilbride
Ohio	Erin O'Reilly
PENNSYLVANIA	LIZ SHOVLIN
Peterborough	Michelle Moffat
San Francisco	Anne Walsh
Sydney	Maureen Tangney
Toronto	Laura Waller
Tralee	Doreen Collins
Washington	Maureen Lynch
Waterford	Enda Jackson

1979

BELFAST	MARITA MARRON
Birmingham	Caroline Deehan
Boston	Margaret Sullivan
Chicago	Angela Mannion
Cork	Joan Whyte
Dublin	Avril Ryan
Florida	Eileen Dorsey
Galway	Annette Rhatighan
Cailín Gaelach	Moire Ní Chéide
Holyoke	Corinne Baker
Jersey	Jacqueline Mandel
Kerry	Josephine Reidy
Las Vegas	Aleasha Magleby
Leeds	Linda Kelly
Limerick	Colette Stephenson

London	Mary O'Connor
Melbourne	Maria O'Brien
Michigan	Brenda Foley
New York	Kerry Whitaker
New Zealand	Christine Bell
Ohio	Mary Jordan
Pennsylvania	Maureen Sullivan
Peterborough	Tracey Stewart
San Francisco	Lynette Kelly
South Wales	Lorraine John
Sydney	Margaret Crowley
Toronto	Catherine O'Halloran
Tralee	Eleanor Carrick
Washington D.C.	Katie Ryan
Waterford	Margaret Hogan

1980

Belfast	Erica Turk
Birmingham	Attracta Hannelly
Boston	Mary Deery
Chicago	Julie Ryan
Cork	Grace Daly
Dublin	Linda Stevens
GALWAY	SHEILA O'HANRAHAN
Holyoke	Patricia Long
Jersey	Olive Corkery
Kerry	Helen Riney
Leeds	Patricia Tolan
Limerick	Barbara Wall
London	Bernadette Lynch
Manchester	Debbie O'Brien
Melbourne	Adele Hanafin
Michigan	Cheryl Collins
New York	Maureen Keegan
Ohio	Julie O'Keeffe
Pennsylvania	Catherine Farnan
Peterborough	Jeanie McCarthy
San Francisco	Sarah Newson
South Wales	Deborah Moriarty
Sydney	Deborah O'Neill
Toronto	Irene Gilligan
Tralee	Kay Costelloe
Washington D.C.	Maureen Kathleen Costelloe
Waterford	Anne McGee
Zimbabwe	Lesley O'Connell

1981

Belfast	Grainne Murrin
Belgium	Wendy Lauvers
BIRMINGHAM & MIDLANDS	DEBORAH CAREY
Boston	Kathleen Ritchie

112

Cork	Fionnuala O'Sullivan
Dublin	Catherine O'Connor
Florida	Tamara Mize
Galway	Joan McGarry
Holyoke	Ann Dean
Jersey	Catherine Gairgain
Kerry	Mary O'Shea
Leeds	Eileen Bayshaw
Limerick	Shirley Bennett
London	Veronica McGowan
Manchester	Ann Marie Carroll
Melbourne	Shaunagh McEvoy
Michigan	Joan Cowley
New York	Donna Kane
Ohio	Maureen Gannon
Pennsylvania	Rosemary Doughtery
Peterborough	Kathleen Fox
San Francisco	Brigid Byrne
South Wales	Melissa Andrews
Sydney	Elizabeth Oldroyd
Thames Valley	Helen McDonnell
Toronto	Kathleen Looney
Tralee	Cicely Kelleher
Washington D.C.	Denise Boland
Waterford	Marian Ryan

1982

Belfast	Linda McKeown
Birmingham	Caroline Lane
Boston	Eleanor Conlon
Brussels	Ann Curtin
Chicago	Kathy Feeney
Cork	Kay Cosgrave
Dublin	Valerie White
Florida	Meg Hartnett
Galway	Geraldine Durkin
Glasgow	Helen Ward
Holyoke	Patti O'Connor
Jersey	Rachel Pipon
Kerry	Annette Whyte
Las Vegas	Cheryl Harvey
Leeds	Maureen McCormack
Limerick	Eileen O'Donoghue
London	Christine Groarke
Melbourne	Kathy Kelly
Manchester	Sarah Tierney
Michigan	Shirley Burne
New York	Maria Hickey
New Zealand	Pauline Larkin
Ohio	Susie Barrett
Pennsylvania	Kathleen Joyce

PETERBOROUGH	LAURA GAINEY
San Francisco	Patty Hayes
South Wales	Frances Slater
Sydney	Emer McDonagh
Thames Valley	Trish Donnelly
Toronto	Anne O'Neill
Tralee	Charlotte O'Neill
Washington	Colleen Curran
Waterford	Philomena Noonan

1983

Adelaide	Maureen Stokes
Belfast	Anita Browne
Boston	Eileen McDonough
Chicago	Sheila Ryan
Cork	Irene De Leeuir
Dublin	Tina McDonnell
Florida	Colleen Finlan
Galway	Celine Mullins
Glasgow	Kathleen McGonigle
Jersey	Carol Hickey
Kerry	Peggy King
Las Vegas	Megan Waterman
Leeds	Eileen Torley
Limerick	Noelle Westropp Bennett
London	Geraldine Geelan
Manchester	Eileen Hanlon
Melbourne	Elizabeth Chambers
Michigan	Patricia Rahilly
Midlands, UK	Jacqueline Hetherington
New York	Noreen Kelly
New Zealand	Bauble Murray
Ohio	Teresa Sammon
Pennsylvania	Jane Irwin
Peterborough	Maureen Condon
San Francisco	Margie Scanlon
South Wales	Christina Wassall
Sydney	Sharon Lynch
Toronto	Mary Watt
Tralee	Martina Keane
Washington D.C.	Margo McNerney
WATERFORD	BRENDA HYLAND

1984

Belfast	Janet Donaghey
Boston	Andrea Griffin
Chicago	Mary Moran
Cork	Noelle Morrison
Dublin	Teresa Macklin
Galway	Mary Conroy
Jersey	Jane Henderson

Kerry   Kathryn Power
Las Vegas   Kathleen Little
Leeds   Mary McGowan
LIMERICK   DIANE HANNAGAN
Manchester   Mary McNeice
Melbourne   Marita Hurry
Memphis   Patricia Lantrip
Michigan   Mary Harrington
Midlands, U.K.   Julia Curran
New York   Eileen Royers
New Zealand   Louise Fitzgerald
Ohio   Carol Mackin
Pennsylvania   Maureen Flynn
Peterborough   Susan Heffernan
S.E. England   Lisa Hill
San Francisco   Sheila Lawlor
Southern California   Imelda Kelly
South Wales   Elizabeth Lawlor
Sydney   Geraldine Stevens
Toronto   Tracey McKenna
Tralee   Sheila O'Mahony
Washington D.C.   Maureen Conroy
Waterford   Rosemary O'Leary

1985

Belfast   Michelle Green
BOSTON   HELENA RAFFERTY
Chicago   Michelle McCormack
Cork   Jane O'Hagan
Darwin   Mary Jane Scanlan
Dallas   Allison Duaine
Dublin   Geraldine Shesgreen
Galway   Bernice O'Rourke
Jersey   Muriel Bowen
Kerry   Michelle Moriarty
Las Vegas   Mimi McGee
Leeds   Joanne McBride
Limerick   Catherine Delaney
Manchester   Ann Marie Giblin
Melbourne   Julia Allen
Midlands U.K.   Perrine Phipps
Michigan   Margaret Riordan
New York   Mary Ann McGuinness
New Zealand   Vivienne McKevitt
Ohio   Jean Masin
Pennsylvania   Kathleen King
Petersborough   Phyllis Vail
San Francisco   Niamh O'Flaherty
S.E. England   Anne Marie Doyle
South California   Kathleen McCarthy
South Wales   Carol McCormack

Sydney   Roseanne Galway
Toronto   Michelle McDonnell
Tralee   Maria O'Connor
Tenerife   Paola Ann Agnew
Washington D.C.   Carrion Swiger
Waterford   Maria Sheehan

1986

Adelaide   Finola McTaggart
Belfast   Siobhan Browne
Boston   Tara O'Brien
Chicago   Maureen Hickey
Cork   Liz Fenton
Dallas   Kathleen Walsh
Darwin   Nikiki Walford
Dublin   Marie Dowling
Galway   Caroline Cawley
Jersey   Anne O'Shea
Kerry   Claire Thompson
Las Vegas   Natalie de Lucia
LEEDS   NOREEN CASSIDY
Limerick   Elaine Mulch
Manchester   Grainne Casey
Melbourne   Joanne Davis
Midlands   Jacqui Duffy
Montreal   Rosaleen Carroll
New York   Kelly Moran
New Zealand   Bronagh Moloney
Peterborough   Julie Sullivan
San Francisco   Sandra Green
Southern California   Debbie McConville
South Wales   Ashley Mulcahy
South West England   Denise Flannery
Sydney   Rita Malone
Toronto   Anne Scott
Tralee   Liz Keane
Washington D.C.   Trish Harkins
Waterford   Louise Whittle

1987

Adelaide   Marianne Blute
Belfast   Grainne Boyle
Boston   Shannon Maura Dalton
Belgium   Patricia Sicora
CHICAGO   LARNA CANOY
Cork   Maria Dunne
Dallas   Molly Regan
Darwin   Olga O'Connor
Dublin   Anne Maria Holland
Galway   Marian Skehill
Jersey C.I.   Marianne Moran

Kerry	Marie O'Dowd
Las Vegas	Eileen James
Leeds	Paula Andrews
Limerick	Majella Murphy
Manchester	Sheila Brady
Melbourne	Regina Hoare
Midlands U.K.	Deirdre Finnegan
Montreal	Janice Campbell
New Zealand	Delwyn Slattery
New York	Jeanette Nealon
Perth	Tara Hannan
Peterborough	Kathleen Norman
Sydney	Donna Goodwin
San Francisco	Marie Ann Nugent
South East England	Karoline McLaughlin
South Wales	Karen O'Flynn
Southern California	Kelly Kathleen Learman
Toronto	Mary O'Connor
Tralee	Nora Sheehy
Washington D.C.	Janice Duffy
Waterford	Siobhan Kierans

1988

Adelaide	Siobhan Dennehy
Belgium	Catherine Lelie
Boston	Christine Golden
Brisbane	Carmel Mulhern
Chicago	Jean-Michael Conroy
Cork	Elaine Ryan
Darwin	Jonelle Doherty
Dublin	Marianne Hurley
Galway	Ann Dooley
Germany	Nadja Konig
Jersey, C. L.	Louise Neiland
Kerry	Mary Lucey
Las Vegas	Kathleen Colbert
Leeds	Marie Mulrennan
Limerick	Carmel Fitzgerald
Manchester	Mary Mulvenna
Melbourne	Sinead O'Sullivan
Midlands, UK	Amanda Griffin
New York	Kathleen O'Gara
NEW ZEALAND	MARY-ANN MURPHY
Perth	Michelle Dealtry
Peterborough	Pauline O'Brien
San Francisco	Sharon Whelan
Southern California	Christine Briers
South-East England	Eileen Dalton
South Wales	Karen Carr
Sydney	Suzanne Barnaville
Toronto	Joanne Rumball

Tralee	Siobhan Fitzgerald
Washington	Teresa McAuliffe
Waterford	Heather Scanlon

1989

Adelaide	Catherine Holdcroft
Belgium	Tara de Coninick
Boston	Kathleen Houlihan
Brisbane	Allannah Mahony
Chicago	Anne Marie McGarry
Cork	Anna Marie Clarke
Darwin	Tamara Field
DUBLIN	SINEAD BOYLE
France	Camille Duconte
Galway	Anne Connelly
Germany	Moya Graf
Jersey, C.I.	Honey Clarke
Kerry	Helen Spillane
Las Vegas	Renee Reuther
Leeds	Wendy Durkan
Limerick	Audrey O'Reilly
Manchester	Caroline Rowley
Melbourne	Lydia Cagney
Midlands UK	Mary Delaney
New York	Colleen Walsh
New Zealand	Louise Glazer
Perth	Orla McKnight
Peterborough	Breda Kelly
San Francisco	Ann O'Brien
South-East England	Caroline Dempsey
Southern California	Colleen Cutler
South Wales	Tracy Griffiths
Switzerland	Vreni Bleiker
Sydney	Catherine Coleman
Texas	Tricia Leahy
Toronto	Gretta Murphy
Ulster	Fiona McGale
Washington D.C.	Ciara Durkan
Waterford	Harryet Hoff

1990

Belgium	Raffaella Sola
Boston	Eileen Leahy
Brisbane	Tracy Walsh
Chicago	Linda Scannell
Cork	Fiona Ring
Darwin	Jane Errity
Dublin	Fionnuala Greene
France	Sophie Baumann
Galway	Una McGath
Jersey	Michelle Dundon

Kerry	Michelle King
Leeds	Caroline Cunningham
Limerick	Adele O'Carroll
Manchester	Tina Fallon
Melbourne	Simone Thomson
Midlands, U. K.	Maria Stanley
New York	Anne Atkinson
New Zealand	Catherine Hogan
Perth	Teresa McGorry
San Francisco	Aileen Kilgariff
South East England	Siobhan Sargeant
Southern California	Shandon Eales
South Wales	Jane Killeen
Switzerland	Sabina Schwarz
Sydney	Kathleen Farrell
Texas	Kelly Leach
Toronto	Vanessa Toland
Ulster	Jean Galligan
Washington D.C.	Margo Ragan
Waterford	Maria Curtin
WEST GERMANY	JULIA DAWSON

1991

Adelaide	Lisa Heatley
Belgium	Linda Donnelly
Boston	Peggy Walsh
Chicago	Kathleen Zeng
CORK	DENISE MURPHY
Darwin	Jane O'Brien
Dublin	Sarah Moore
France	Simone Cahill
Galway	Anna-Maria O'Sullivan
Germany	Ciara Byrne
Jersey	Tricia Fagan
Kerry	Dympna Buckely
Las Vegas	Brigid Little
Leeds	Gabby Jorath
Limerick	Anne O'Toole
Manchester	Lisa Cryan
Melbourne	Rachel Clarke
Midlands U.K.	Leanora Conmey
New York	Patricia Prendergast
New Zealand	Sinead O'Hanlon
Perth	Suzanne Colwell
Queensland	Tricia McGirl
S.E. England	Vovien Nolan
San Francisco	Nora Cotter
Southern California	Mary Pat Shields
South Wales	Petrina Egan
Sydney	Shauna Kelly
Texas	Monica Ryan

Toronto	Sharon Mailey
Ulster	Sinead Murphy
Washington D.C.	Maura McElhenny
Waterford	Lorraine Kehoe

1992

Adelaide	Aideen Campbell
Belgium	Katia McDermott
Boston	Lisa Marie Bailey
Chicago	Tamara McDonough
Cork	Rachelle O'Neill
Darwin	Anne Louise Hartree
Dublin	Lisa Corley
France	Anne Marie Brassil
GALWAY	NIAMH GROGAN
Germany	Iris Friedrich
Jersey	Gabrielle Kelly
Kerry	Catherine McCarthy
Leeds	Carleen Brennan
Limerick	Una Slattery
Manchester	Teresa Donnelly
Melbourne	Rosaleen Clarke
Midlands U.K.	Nina Rawson
New Orleans	Jennifer Susan Coleman
New York	Mary Anne Connaughton
New Zealand	Andrea Helena Murray
Perth	Dania Marie Lynch
Queensland	Sharon James
S.E. England	Paula Collins
San Francisco	Noreen McGee
	(replaced by Jennifer Doyle Lopez)
South California	Kari Ann Patterson
South Wales	Michelle Gallagher
Sydney	Tonia Walsh
Texas	Cathleen Ruther Naftzger
Toronto	Maura Alicia Matesic
Ulster	Una Glass
Washington D.C.	Bridget Karkins
Waterford	Heather Roche

1993

Adelaide	Michele Murphy
Belgium	Annemarie Lynch
Boston	Kelly Dailey
Chicago	Maureen Finnegan
Cork	Fiona White
Darwin	Sheila Burton
Dublin	Mary Corkery
France	Orla Flynn
Galway	Deirdre May
Germany	Sabina Sheehan

Jersey	Patricia Spain
Kerry	Trudi O'Sullivan
Leeds	Charlotte Walker
Limerick	Osyth O'Flaherty
Manchester	Selina Griffin
Melbourne	Jacqueline Fahy
MIDLANDS U.K.	KIRSTY FLYNN
New Orleans	Kathleen Shea
New York	Kelly-Anne McGrath
New Zealand	Rachel Jane Bryce
Perth	Pamela Magill
Queensland	Bernadette Skehan
S.E. England	Una O'Shea
San Francisco	Doreen Cummins
South California	Eileen Hunt
South Wales	Liz Nihan
Sydney	Susan O'Neill
Texas	Maureen Kelly
Toronto	Jennifer Daly
Ulster	Jacinta McMahon
Washington D.C.	Victoria Anderson
Waterford	Evon Kelly

1994

Adelaide	Sinead Sheehy
Belgium	Sharon De Weerdt
Boston	Jennifer O'Mahoney Braffitt
Chicago	Maura Farrell
Cork	Emillie Pickering
Darwin	Ursula Carolyn
Dubai	Niamh Staunton
Dublin	Fiona Cullen
France	Evelyne Faye
Galway	Nuala Cahill
Germany	Una Conroy
Jersey	Therese Walsh
Kerry	Colette O'Halloran
Leeds	Karen Jordan
LIMERICK	MUIRNE HURLEY
Manchester	Bernadette Rogers
Melbourne	Janina Lawless
Midlands U.K.	Martina Raynes
New Orleans	Katherine Schexnayder
New York	Carolyn Reilly
New Zealand	Linda McFetridge
Perth	Eileen Milligan
Queensland	Ingrid Holohan
S.E. England	Clare Kavanagh
San Francisco	Melinda Miller
South California	Katherine Geary
South Wales	Marguerite Riordan

Sydney	Geraldine Costello
Texas	Shannon Higgins
Toronto	Deirdre Brett
Ulster	Alison Mulholland
Washington D.C.	Jeanine Cummins

1995

Adelaide	Claire Driver
Belgium	Arlene Daniels
Boston	Laura Olsen
Chicago	Frances Sheehan
Cork	Sinead McCluskey
Darwin	Alison Devine
Dubai	Maeve Devery
Dublin	Marie Monks
France	Marie O'Callaghan
Galway	Marie Eilis Ní Fhlatharta
Germany	Maureen Kaiser
Jersey	Siobhan Murtagh
Kerry	Honor Hurley
Leeds	Yvonne Heffernan
Limerick	Fidelma O'Sullivan
London & S.E. England	Mary Carmody
Manchester	Jennifer Crampton
Melbourne	Jacqui Hope
Midlands U.K.	Rosaleen McHugh
New Orleans	Megan O'Neil
New York	Mary Lynn Collins
New Zealand	Chantelle McCabe
PERTH	NYOMI HORGAN
Queensland	Caroline Carpenter
San Francisco	Erin Sorensen
South Africa	Victoria McLaren
South California	Therese Sullivan
South Wales	Jacinta Hargan
Sydney	Fionna Ward
Texas	Jennifer Doherty
Toronto	Tara Lester
Ulster	Michelle Maguire
Washington D.C.	Carroll Herr
Waterford	Miriam Carey

1996

Adelaide	Genevieve O'Reilly
Belgium	Lesa McCann
Boston & New England	Sinead Cassidy
Chicago	Noreen Cunnie
Cork	Helen O'Sullivan
Darwin	Rondelle Miatke
Dubai	Lorah O'Malley
Dublin	Yvonne Temple

France	Denise Brown
Galway	Lorraine Cunniffe
Jersey	Natalie O'Sullivan
Kerry	Geraldine O'Brien
Leeds	Frances Grogan
Limerick	Yvonne Cleary
London & South England	Caroline O'Donnell
Manchester	Emma Murphy
Melbourne	Fiona O'Brien
Midlands U.K.	Lisa Judge
New Orleans	Melissa Brick
New York	Veronica Sheehan
New Zealand	Catherine Wallace
Perth	Caroline Windsor
Queensland	Samantha Andrew
San Francisco	Karyn C. Donnelly
South Africa	Samantha Byrne
South California	Margaret Malone
South Wales	Colette Botto
Sydney	Melissa Fahey
Texas	Molly McMurry
TORONTO	COLLEEN MOONEY
Ulster	Rosemarie Howden
Washington D.C.	Tara O'Connor
Waterford	Geraldine O'Shea

1997

Boston - New England	Sorcha O'Sullivan
Chicago	Amy McCarthy Supak
Cork	Sinead Curtin
Darwin	Raelene Ann Blackmore
Dubai	Niamh (Eilish) Cassidy
Dublin	Elizabeth (Lisa) McGowan
FRANCE	SINEAD LONERGAN
Galway	Colette Mary Ansbro
Jersey	Ann O'Sullivan
Kerry	Hazel Griffin
Leeds	Georgina Burke
Limerick	Audrey Jennifer Dooley
London & South England	Michelle Lyttle
Manchester	Siobhan Madonna Madden
Melbourne	Emily Elliott
Midlands U.K.	Kerry O'Connell
New Orleans	Margaret Rose McMahon
New York	Melissa Ann Clare
New Zealand	Michelle Mulholland
Perth	Lynda Lee Smyth
Queensland	Alexis Wavell-Smith
San Francisco	Maureen Sinclair
South Africa	Skye Stevenson
South California	Saroj Verma

South Wales	Beth Alexandra Mulcahy
Sydney	Yvette Jennifer McCloghry
Texas	Malley Jean McCoy
Toronto	Jacqueline Leggett Nugent
U.K. Midlands	Kerry O'Carroll
Ulster	Lucia Cleary
Washington D.C.	Jeanne Frances Monahan
Waterford	Ruth Mary O'Connor

1998

Belgium	Elizabeth Casey
Boston - New England	Keira Flynn
Chicago	Alison Chrstine Davia
Cork	Audrey Mongan
Darwin	Heidi Trobbiani
Dubai	Caroline Bailey
Dublin	Frances Carley
GALWAY	LUZVEMINDA O'SULLIVAN
Kerry	Rebekah Wall
Leeds	Siobhan Harrington
Limerick	Aileen O'Callaghan
London & South England	Catherine Orr
Manchester	Ann Marie Mohan
Melbourne	Cindi Connell
Midlands U.K.	Emma Hyland
New Orleans	Patricia Anne Warren
New York	Kathleen McMahon
New Zealand	Nicole Smith
Perth	Nichola Margaret Renton
Queensland	Maria Stella Crealey
San Francisco	Denise Michelle Engler
South Africa	Bronwyn Millar
South California	Allison McGuire
South Wales	Joanne Marie Halloran
Sydney	Kylie Anne Burke
Texas	Caroline Wilson
Toronto	Siobhan Hurley
U.K. Midlands	Emma Hyland
Ulster	Amanda Dunne
Washington D.C.	Emilia Saunders
Waterford	Orla Mary Cusack

1999

Belgium	Niamh Connery
Boston - New England	Patricia Lillis
Chicago	Kathryn Anne Killacky
CORK	GERALDINE O'GRADY
Darwin	Patricia Byrne
Dubai	Patricia O'Toole
Dublin	Aoife O'Connor
France	Fiona Carville

Galway	Olivia Burke
Japan	Amanda Ryan
Kerry	Helen Ahern
Leeds	Ann Murray
Limerick	Joanne Behan
London & South England	Marie McGrath
Manchester	Eleanor McGovern
Melbourne	Genevieve Brannigan
Midlands U.K.	Carly Jones
New Orleans	Briget Hope
New York	Valerie Burke
New Zealand	Bridget Hope
Perth	Erin Lee Chen
Queensland	Angela Marie Martin
San Francisco	Colleen Melissa Normon
South Africa	Eileen Donaldson
South California	Kerry O'Connell
South Wales	Clare Attwell
Sydney	Orla Tonge
Texas	Sandra Strouse
Toronto	Danielle Sweeney
U.K. Midlands	Carly Jones
Ulster	Jennifer McConville
Washington D.C.	Mary McFadden
Waterford	Vanessa Brophy

2000

Belgium	Tracey Culleton
Boston	Karen Kierce
Chicago	Moira O'Connor-Curren
Cork	Carol Anthony
Darwin	Bridget McQuaid
Dubai	Claire Ward
Dublin	Louise Elizabeth Kerr
Galway	Evelyn O'Connor
Japan	Tara Wakely
Kerry	Naomi O'Connor
Limerick	Olive Geary
Melbourne	Tara Glynn
New Orleans	Gara Lynn Gorenflo
NEW YORK	ROISIN EGENTON
New Zealand	Catherine Goodwin
Perth	Louise Lowery
Queensland	Liesel Bremhorst
San Francisco	Kerry Cooper
South Africa	Fiona Tobin
South Australia	Jessica O'Donnell
South California	Erin McCreary
Sydney	Gabrielle Wells
Texas	Julia Dohm
Toronto	Sarah Duncan

Ulster	Lisa Hyndman
United Kingdom	Kelly Ann McNally
Washington	Alison Marie
Waterford	Aileen Nolan

2001

Belgium	Maria Byrne
Boston & New England	Sinead Bridget Stewart
Chicago	Claire O'Connor
Cork	Olivia Walsh
Darwin	Tiffany Luck
Dubai	Sarah Howard
Dublin	Fiona Burne
Galway	Ruth Smith
Kerry	Linda O'Sullivan
Limerick	Paula Glynn
Melbourne	Mairead Dundas
New Orleans	Kimberly Talley
New York	Katherine Towne
New Zealand	Katherine McMahon
PERTH	LISA MANNING
Ros Fodhla	Rosemarie Ní Leathlobhair
San Francisco	Sorcha Byrne
South Africa	Melisa Cross
South Australia	Aimee Butler
South California	Cameo McMillan
Sydney	Caitriona Hayes
Texas	Maura Brown
Ulster	Sheila Patton
United Kingdom	Siobhan McCullagh
Washington	Gretchen Learman
Waterford	Clare Sheriff

2002

Boston	Aisling O'Sullivan
Cork	Deirdre Coughlan
Darwin	Cheryl Willoughby
Dubai	Zena Al-Nazer
Dublin	Claire Roche
Galway	Karen Broderick
ITALY	TAMARA GERVASONI
Kerry	Olivia Buckley
Limerick	Sheila English
Luxembourg	Yvonne Linterr
Melbourne	Jennifer Menon
New Orleans	Paige Egan
New York	Shireen Ruth Russell
New Zealand	Vivien Lynch
Perth	Kelly O'Shaughnessy
Philadelphia	Noreen Donahue
Queensland	Mellisa Hickey

Ros Fodhla	Eibhlin Ní Choistealbha
San Francisco	Erin Lucey
South California	Anneliese Schumacher
Sydney	Fiona Tuite
Texas	Ashley Childress
Toronto	Charlotte Wilkinson
Ulster	Mairead Greene
United Kingdom	Nicola Norris
Washington	Joy Peck
Waterford	Beth Condon

2003

Boston	Grainne Lanigan
Cork	Joanna O'Keeffe
Darwin	Jess McNeill
Dubai	Celina Cusack
DUBLIN	ORLA TOBIN
England	Charlotte Doherty
Galway	Aoife Mulholland
Kerry	Jessie Lyons
Limerick	Petula Martyn
Luxembourg	Deborah Maher
New Orleans	Katherine Duckworth
New York	Kathleen Tuohy
New Zealand	Katherine Kelly
Perth	Rachel Ragan
Philadelphia	Sheena Trainer
Queensland	Cara Maher
Ros Fodhla	Blathnaid Ní Nuallain
San Francisco	Siobhan McDonagh
South Australia	Edel Ryan
South California	Corinna Zeter
Sydney	Holly Lowe
Texas	Stephanie Farmer
Toronto	Cat McCormick
Ulster	Ciara McGinley
Washington D.C.	Orla Cahalane
Waterford	Sarah Gladney

2004

Boston & New England	Caitlin Monahan
Cork	Ruth Kenneally
Darwin	Courtney Hare
Dubai	Louise Smith
Dublin	Joanna Cullen
England	Angela Crowley
Galway	Sarah McCartan
Kerry	Olivia Dineen
Kildare	Victoria Barry
KILKENNY	ORLA O'SHEA
Laois	Anna Maria Hogan

Limerick	Yvonne Nagle
Luxembourg	Eileen Byrne
New Orleans	Colleen McKay
New York	Elizabeth Kee
Perth	Katherine White
Philadelphia	Sinead De Roiste
Queensland	Sophie Cleary
Ros Fodhla	Máire Ní Ghiollabhain
San Francisco	KC McCabe
South Australia	Pamela Relihan
South California	Suzanne Paine
Sydney	Lucy Doris
Texas	Caitlin Lowry
Toronto	Kate Heffernon
Ulster	Michaela Harte
Washington D.C.	Meaghan Donovan
Waterford	Lisa Kavanagh

2005

Belfast	Martina Murray
Boston &New England	Ellen Pyzik
Carlow	Maura Murphy
Clare	Blathnaid O'Donoghue
Cork	Deborah Barrett
Darwin	Shannon Byrne
Dubai	Rachel Barrett
Dublin	Elena McGivney
Kildare	Gillian Doyle
Kerry	Siobhan Ryan
Leitrim	Pamela Bourke
Limerick	Catriona Dwane
London	Charlene Foley
Luxembourg	Jane Bretin
MAYO	AOIBHINN NÍ SHÚILLEABHÁIN
Midlands U.K.	Kerrie Doherty
New Orleans	Jenna Burke
New York	Caitlin Burke
New Zealand	Esther Budding
North West England	Roisin Corry
Perth	Fiona Stokes
Philadelphia	Karen Boyce
Queensland	Michelle Emery
San Francisco	Katie Watts
South Australia	Laura Watson
Southern California	Ashley Stanbury
Sydney	Cristin McCloskey
Texas	Molly Kealy
Toronto	Caitlyn McCann
Washington D.C.	Kate Riley

2006

Armagh	Blathnaid Carlin
Belfast	Aisling McDowell
Boston & New England	Caitlin Sullivan
Clare	Theresa Roseingrave
Cork	Patricia Cotter
Darwin	Brigit Killen
Derry	Catherine Peiples
Dubai	Maria Curtin
Dublin	Sarah Guilmartin
Kerry	Colleen Shannon
Limerick	Mary Sheahan
London	Grainne Canny
Luxembourg	Leath Freeman
Midlands U.K	Holly McGuire
New Orleans	Dorian Joyce
New York	Melisa Teelin
New Zealand	Emma Coffey
North West England	Ciara Toner
Perth	Aishling Reid
Philadelphia	Christine Frawley
QUEENSLAND	KATHRYN FEENY
Ros Fodhla	Áine Ní Sheibhin
San Francisco	Aislin Roche
South Australia	Niamh O'Reilly
South California	Meghan Dixon
Sydney	Laura Jean Bradley
Texas	Erin Barnard
Toronto	Jemma Lee Creelman
Washington D.C.	Carolyn Kirwin
Westmeath	Edel O'Connor

2007

Birmingham	Aimee Porch
Boston & New England	Nora Rafferty
Cork	Mary Rose Howell
Darwin	Kate Ó Fathartai
Derry	Niamh O'Kane
Dubai	Aileen McCarthy
Dublin	Aoife Judge
Fermanagh	Aisling Reihill
France	Madeleine Barry
Kerry	Laura Costelloe
Limerick	Melanie Carroll
Liverpool	Grace Kelly
London	Katie Crean
Longford	Grainne Fox
Luxembourg	Jackie Maher
Newcastle-Upon Tyne	Norette Kearney
New Orleans	Rosie Dempre
NEW YORK	LISA MURTAGH
New Zealand	Sarah Dwyer
Perth	Orla Neff
Philadelphia	Colleen Gallagher
Queensland	Talia Evans
San Francisco	Katie Van Bogart
South California	Aileen Whelan
Texas	Meagan Foley
Toronto	Sarah Nester
Washington D.C.	Laura Olsen
Westmeath	Marisa Murray
Wicklow	Lisa Maria Berry

2008

Boston & New England	Cailyn McDermott
Cavan	Mairead Lyng
Cork	Niamh O'Hanlon
Coventry	Gemma Hughes
Darwin	Kate Hodspith
Derry	Catherine Lagan
Dubai	Emma Dwane
Dublin	Hannah McDonnell
Kerry	Katie Nolan
Kildare	Denise Healy
Liverpool	Fiona McConnell
London	Belinda Brown
Louth	Karol-Ann Keenan
Luxembourg	Heidi Connolly
New Jersey	Rita Talty
New Orleans	Leah Boyer
New York	Ellen Condon
New Zealand	Aislinn Ryan
Newcastle-Upon-Tyne	Aoife Dowdall
Perth	Sarah Partridge
Philadelphia	Colleen Tully
Queenslanad	Harlie Byrnes
Roscommon	Triona O'Connor
San Francisco	Jamie Lundy
South Australia	Leer McDlenaghan
Southern California	Sinead Cunningham
Sydney	Hannah Bradley
Texas	Rosin Mulligan
TIPPERARY	AOIFE KELLY
Toronto	Karina Higgins
Washington D.C.	Maureen Hassen

The Yellow Rose of Texas

An Officer and a Gentleman

The Darwin Rose, A Vision in Pink

CAN YOU NAME THE ROSE?

2006 Rose Kathryn Feeney with ten Roses of Tralee from earlier years

'Escorts must be unattached, a complete gentleman (but with a wicked sense of humour), well mannered (but with a touch of the devil), aged between 21 and 30, and above all must know how to treat a lady!' *from the 'Men Wanted' ad for the 2009 Festival*

Top: 1994 Escorts
Left: 1996 Escorts; right; 1998 Escorts

T. RYLE DWYER is a regular columnist with the *Irish Examiner* and an historian with more than twenty books on different aspects of Irish history. He was educated at Tralee CBS and university in the USA, where he earned a doctorate at the University of North Texas. Margaret Dwyer, his mother, was a member of the original committee of the Festival of Kerry in 1959 and was Honorary Secretary and a President of the organization so he had an inside view of the festival over many years.

First published 2009 by The O'Brien Press Ltd,
12 Terenure Road East, Rathgar, Dublin 6, Ireland.
Tel: +353 1 4923333; Fax: +353 1 4922777
E-mail: books@obrien.ie
Website: www.obrien.ie

ISBN: 978-1-84717-177-1

A catalogue record for this title is available from The British Library

1 2 3 4 5 6 7 8 9 10
09 10 11 12 13 14 15

Typesetting, layout, editing, design: The O'Brien Press Ltd
Printing: GPS Colour Graphics Ltd

Picture Credits: All photographs by kind permission of *The Kerryman*, except for pages 49, 55, 56, 61, 93, 94, 95, 96, 97, 98, 99(top), 100, 103, by permission of the *Irish Examiner*; pages 4(top), 23, 27, 40(top), 61(top), 69(bottom), 78, 90(bottom right), 97(top), 99(bottom), 101, 102, 107, 124, 125, 127, and back cover(top), courtesy of Joe Hanley; page 64 (top)courtesy of John Cleary, pages 7(bottom), 33(bottom), 87(top), courtesy of Domnick Walsh; page 1 and 103 (bottom) courtesy of Mark O'Sullivan.
Inside cover images courtesy of Sheila Carroll, CREATIVE REPUBLIC